ARE THE KEYS
IN THE FREEZER?

AN ADVOCATE'S GUIDE
FOR ALZHEIMER'S AND OTHER DEMENTIAS

PATRICI..JERI WARNER

ISBN: 1492927449

ISBN 13: 9781492927440

Library of Congress Control Number: 2013919900
CreateSpace Independent Publishing Platform
North Charleston, South Carolina

This book is dedicated to our mother,
who continued to teach us about life,
even when she could no longer speak.

DISCLAIMER

The interpretation of documents, opinions, and viewpoints expressed in this book are solely those of the authors. The choice of material and emphasis on particular subject matter is based on the authors' personal experiences, which may be different for other families. Readers are advised to do independent research on topics of interest and draw their own conclusions. Readers should seek professional advice about the specifics of their loved ones' medical, legal, or regulatory circumstances as they pertain to laws in their own states.

The authors do not have any monetary affiliations with organizations or individuals mentioned in this book. They may not have personally used the services of every organization mentioned. Some organizations described in this book are "for profit," and it is incumbent upon readers to verify products or services independently before making financial transactions. Naming organizations or individuals in this book does not imply an endorsement, referral, or statement about their qualifications or the accuracy of their public information. Contact addresses and telephone numbers were correct at the time of this writing, but may be subject to change.

The views of individuals quoted in this book are solely their own views and not necessarily endorsed by the authors. The authors disclaim any responsibility for actions taken by readers based on legal, medical, or other references and conclusions cited in this book.

ABOUT THE AUTHORS

Pat Woodell, Brenda Niblock, and Jeri Warner are first-time writers in the field of dementia care. The compelling story of their mother's decline into dementia is blended with research, practical insights, and tips for families looking for direction in how to care for aging spouses or parents.

Pat has written numerous technical publications for the Alaska Department of Commerce and Economic Development in Anchorage where she worked for twelve years as a project manager and instructor. After retirement, she volunteered for the Consumer Protection Division in the Washington State Attorney General's Office of Consumer Protection. Pat received a bachelor of arts degree from the University of Washington in Seattle, Washington, with majors in English literature and German literature, and a master's degree in Asian studies from the University of the Philippines in Quezon City, Philippines.

Brenda is a graduate of the University of Oregon in Eugene, Oregon, and holds a master's degree in science and teaching from Portland State University in Portland, Oregon. She is a retired health educator, having advocated for prevention of tobacco use for over two decades. Brenda volunteers as a public speaker and educator for Donate Life Northwest, promoting awareness of the need for more registered organ donors. A transplant survivor herself, Brenda understands the importance of advocacy in medical issues, and uses this experience in her role as a facilitator for a liver transplant support group.

Jeri was a physical therapist for thirty-five years and retired after twenty-one years with Kaiser Permanente in Portland, Oregon. Her focus was orthopedics. She received her bachelor's degree in physical therapy from the University of Washington in Seattle, Washington. Jeri's experience in the health-care field prepared her for working with older adults faced with the physical challenges of aging. Jeri is active in her community and volunteers as an English tutor for adults.

The family's story is based on experiences in a real town and actual care facilities in the Pacific Northwest.

PREFACE

In 2005, when our mother was first diagnosed with dementia, we (her four daughters) knew next to nothing about this disease or any other medical problems affecting the elderly. Our introduction to dementia arrived in the form of a medical crisis in Mom's life. It was followed by a series of events that left clues to a problem, but never a clear understanding about Mom's condition.

Initially, the four of us had trouble finding common ground in making decisions about her care. We had differences of opinion about where she should live, and whether her independent lifestyle would affect her safety. The beginning was rocky, but in the end we were able to compromise.

Arguments and compromise were nothing new to us; Mom had spent most of her parenting years trying to promote goodwill among the four of us. After we left home, she continued using a fine hand to interweave our lives and ensure that we stayed in touch as a family. She organized family gatherings and acted as an intermediary in writing letters and making phone calls about our activities. If she were here today, she would be surprised to know that some twenty-five hundred e-mails about her care had kept us in daily communication for the last five years of her life.

Mom didn't like the idea of facility living, but she would have applauded our approach to looking out for her rights. Our mother was militant about defending her rights, and she was a consumer advocate long before it was fashionable to voice complaints about products and services. She pushed for "the right thing," and she protested loudly and waved her fist at any personal injustice. She would have complimented us for taking an advocate's role in overseeing her health-care and living arrangements. Mom liked to help other people, and we're certain she would be happy that we're sharing our experiences with other families looking for answers about caring for loved ones with Alzheimer's disease or other dementias.

In the process of writing this book, we interviewed professionals in the fields of psychology, law, and medicine. We called on industry experts to help with technical reviews to clear up questions and improve accuracy. We visited facilities with different care philosophies and got their views about changes in the industry. We looked for national resources that would help other families. Two of our reviewers had parents with dementia, and their comments contributed to the subject matter in our book. Our reviewers also encouraged us to speak from the heart about our personal feelings and experiences.

Although our family has medical experience, we began as newcomers to the world of dementia and care facilities. Advice was available from many people along the way, but we didn't grasp the meaning of what was yet to come. Each change in Mom's condition taught us new things about dementia, prompting us to ask new questions and do additional reading. Each change in

Mom's health honed our ability to interpret her needs and resolve issues about her care.

We hope that other families find their own beginnings in our story. Our five-year journey had many rough patches, but just as many rewards. It's all about learning new attitudes and viewpoints, and learning to focus on what families can do to make dementia care a meaningful experience.

ACKNOWLEDGMENTS

In the beginning, our goal was to write a family story about dementia. In the course of our research, that goal changed as we gained insight into the hopes and concerns of the people we met in memory care facilities. These people taught us about patience and consideration for others who are moving through life more slowly but with a grace and dignity that's still beyond our grasp. We reshaped our writing as our understanding about their lives grew, and we hope we've adequately represented the little things that affect their everyday lives.

The opinions of our reviewers also influenced the direction of our writing. Nine people read the preliminary draft of our book, encouraged us in our writing, and shared their expertise with us. We thank them for their help in framing issues and in contributing to the direction of our writing. Our thanks go to Stephen D. Lopez, Jonelle Battaglia, George Byron Wright, Rebecca Ostrom, Cherry Shaw, Lynda Johnson, Connie Kirkpatrick, Vi Schick, and our sister, Leslie Angelo.

We owe a debt of gratitude to the following technical reviewers who shared their time in commenting on our work. Their opinions and professional expertise were invaluable in helping us present our story as accurately as possible. Thanks to Anne E. Koepsell, MHA, BSN, RN, executive director, Washington State Hospice and Palliative Care Organization, for her help with our chapter on hospice and palliative care. We would also like to thank Paul Malley, president, Aging with Dignity, and Susan E. Hickman, PhD, for their comments on advance directives, *Five Wishes,* and Physicians Orders for Life-sustaining Treatment (POLST) forms.

Several long-term care professionals reviewed portions our draft: Toni M. Goins, referral manager/marketing director, Liberty Country Place Skilled Nursing and Rehab; Dorothy Boyd, RN, ADNS, Liberty Country Place; Bruce Dillon, pastor; and Eva Arant, memory care specialist. Mark Kleinman, MD, family physician, helped with questions about medical issues that accompany dementia.

Thanks to Felix Billingsley, PhD, for reviewing our draft and discussing approaches to often-difficult subjects. Patti Good's editorial assistance lightened our load considerably, and we thank her for the many hours she spent helping us get it right.

We're also grateful to Derick Scovel, PhD, president, clinical director, and co-owner of GeroMedical and Scovel Psychological Services. He helped with our opening chapter on dementia and advised us on many topics during the two-year course of our writing. A special thank you goes to the late Tamara Hayes, PhD, for making time to help us during her illness. Tamara offered us resources, new ideas for organizing material, and inspiration. Our book would not have been possible without the help of these people and we are in their debt.

Finally we would like to thank the many people who have written about Alzheimer's and other dementias, contributing to the body of research that continues to educate and inform families. They have added to our own understanding of dementia and have brought clarity to an often difficult subject.

INTRODUCTION

*"My mother came home from work, opened the freezer
to take out a beef roast, put her car keys in the freezer, and
took the roast to the bedroom."*

Daughter of a night-shift nurse, June 2010

It's frightening, isn't it? As we get older, many of us misplace things without realizing it. Sometimes we walk into a room and forget why we went there. Little shreds of doubt about memory problems begin to chip away at our self-confidence. What if these incidents begin to happen more frequently? Should we tell someone? See someone? Or should we keep our doubts to ourselves? Whom do we talk to about memory problems?

We're often reluctant to discuss our fears about memory problems because they're viewed with preju-dice. Fear of the unknown keeps us from seeking medi-cal advice, and many people won't confront a reality that might change their lives in ways they cannot yet imagine. But every day, people we know act on their concerns, and some are diagnosed with Alzheimer's disease or other dementias. These people must redefine their lives as they come to terms with how dementia will affect their futures.

As a nation of families, it's time to face the reality that dementia may intrude on the ordinary lives of people just like us. Presently, some twenty million people are caring for 5.4 million others with this devastating disease. In the United States alone, the numbers are growing: about 13.8 million people will be affected by Alzheimer's disease and other dementias in the next three and a half decades.[1] Ninety percent of these people will spend their final months or years in a care facility.

Our mother was part of the care-facility population for five years, an experience that redefined our thinking about dementia care and prompted us to look at care issues more closely. When we searched for solutions to our questions, we were confronted with mountains of data and a learning curve so steep that it was hard to find a starting point.

The body of research about dementia care offers an overwhelming amount of guidance, statistics, and opinions on almost any topic. While much of it is helpful, information is revised continuously, and it is colored by conflicting political and social issues. Laws that regulate the care industry vary from state to state, and they change all the time. Because of all this uncertainty, it's undeniable that families will still continue to ask the same questions about dementia care over and over again.

How do families sift through all this advice and determine what's relevant to them and their loved ones? Our book, *Are the Keys in the Freezer?* answers some of these questions. It steps beyond ordinary government pamphlets, advice from nonprofit organizations, and pages of medical research about dementia. It follows the course of our family's decisions over five years, offers insight into the care choices we made, and describes the outcome of those choices. *Are the Keys in the Freezer?* is our family's story—a story that examines many basic, yet powerful, issues that we encountered along the way.

These kinds of insights seem to be exactly what's missing from the public conversation about dementia care. Much of what is written today begs an explanation of on-the-ground, day-to-day decision making as it affects the lives of ordinary families. Our book fills that void by describing the choices we made and our reasoning behind them.

Our mother died in the summer of 2011, just two weeks before her eighty-eighth birthday. Now that time has passed, we can look back on events objectively. We learned about dementia by trial and error, and we stumbled many times, because we didn't know where to turn. Now we realize the importance of understanding the course of the disease and its outcome—this knowledge would have given us the tools to plan ahead and provide the best possible care for our mother. The strength of this book, in fact, is the perspective it brings to other families who are faced with problems that seem insurmountable. We hope this book will help others face their questions and fears to prepare for what's yet to come.

The early stages of dementia are a good time to finalize legal documents pertaining to end-of-life care. Advance directives are complex and often difficult documents to interpret. Our research on this topic gave us a new perspective about living wills and the complex choices that lie hidden beneath the surface of their language. *Are the Keys in the Freezer?* reveals surprising information about end-of-life legal documents and their power to affect decisions about end-of-life care.

For those families whose plans include long-term care facilities, careful planning has a big payoff in terms of the cost and quality of care. Our book describes how we selected care facilities and how we planned a budget to ensure that the family had enough money.

Care facility service agreements are surprisingly detailed, and we were caught off guard in the sales office more than once. As a result of our experiences, our book analyzes care facility agreements and highlights issues we think might be of interest to other families. We offer tips for negotiating agreements, and we offer solutions for getting a fair price. We offer ideas for ensuring that services are delivered as promised.

Are the Keys in the Freezer? describes how we prequalified our mother for hospice care before she became eligible for the program. For many families, applying to hospice is a last-minute affair, and precious time is lost in paperwork routines—time that could be spent in getting hospice support and spending time with a loved one. This book touches on how the hospice program worked with us and explains how its staff is organized to help families.

On a positive note, the care industry is undergoing sweeping social and organizational changes. Facility residents are at the center of this storm and stand to benefit greatly from these new ideas. *Are the Keys in the Freezer?* describes how these changes will benefit future generations, and how resources, technologies, and services can help early-dementia patients remain safely in their homes.

Every dementia patient's situation is unique and requires a different approach tailored to her personal circumstances. Good judgment and foresight will determine the success of this approach, and families who are well informed will have the tools to make successful care decisions.

TABLE OF CONTENTS

CHAPTER ONE

COMING TO TERMS WITH DEMENTIA

*"My Memory is getting so bad, I think I have Alzheimer's
Disease. Cheryl [her neighbor] says, 'I do not have that.' She
could be in Denial, but I am not. If I do have it, I want to
know. I asked my Dr. about it and asked her if there was a test
for Alzheimer's Disease. She ordered a Blood Test at the Lab."*

Mom, in a letter dated October 14, 2005, prior
to her diagnosis of dementia.

A northwest breeze blew through the open door,
a welcome respite to the rising temperatures in
the kitchen. Sunlight poured through the windows,
ushering in one of the warmest, driest days of summer.
It was the morning of August 8, 2003, the day of Mom's
eightieth birthday, and party preparations were in full
swing.

The clatter of knives on chopping boards competed with sounds of laughter as we thumbed through recipe books and set out platters of hors d'oeuvres for lunch. Gracie, a slender black Lab, lay sleeping in the corner, oblivious to the loud sixties music pulsing through the kitchen. Mom was at home, no doubt thinking about the upcoming evening with friends and relatives. She would enjoy seeing old friends and family at her party; she had been a widow for thirty years, and her circle had grown smaller as friends passed away or moved to other towns. An eightieth birthday party would attract relatives from far-flung communities, turning the occasion into an extended family reunion.

A ringing phone cut through the noisy kitchen and brought the chatter and music to a sudden standstill. It was Mom—she had just returned home from a visit to the bagel deli and was stumbling through an account of what had happened. She had fallen from a stool onto the concrete reception floor but never completely lost consciousness. Employees had tried to help, but Mom insisted she could drive home. Everything was fine; she simply paused in the deli until she felt better, got in her car, and drove back to her house.

We dropped our knives and rushed Mom to an emergency room. A computerized tomography (CT) scan of her brain revealed that she'd just had a ministroke, and that other small strokes had happened in the past. Mom was shaken, but otherwise okay, and doctors released her into our care. The party went on that evening as planned, and Mom didn't seem to be outwardly affected by this frightening event.

The ministroke was a wake-up call, and we wondered why Mom hadn't reacted to her fall more seriously. The four of us began comparing stories about recent experiences and discovered that we'd all noticed changes in Mom's judgment and behavior. As we pieced together small, unrelated incidents, we realized that little memory lapses had been going on for some time. Mom had mentioned losing her way driving to familiar places. She forgot to wear her glasses on many days, definitely a concern because of her poor vision. But the big tip-off was a midnight phone call to the police, reporting that a long-dead brother had gone to the pharmacy and hadn't returned home. As we learned much later, people with dementia often have vivid dreams that they act on as reality.

A review of Mom's finances revealed problems in other areas of her daily life. Normally a thrifty person, now she was opening her wallet or writing checks for everything and everyone. Checks went out to charitable organizations, which were followed up with phone calls and mailed solicitations for more donations. Mom's credit card statements were filled with magazine subscription purchases that had no relationship to her skills or interests. These things may have happened more often than we were aware of. Without knowing it at the time, we were beginning a very long journey with an unfamiliar disease: dementia.

For some time, we had sensed that something was wrong, but we didn't understand exactly what was happening. No one we knew had experienced these types of problems with a spouse or parent. Dementia was unfamiliar to us, and we had no idea about warning signs. In hindsight, what we thought was age-related forgetfulness was really a mild stage of dementia. Later, we spoke with many people who'd had similar experiences with their own parents. They, too, had recognized their family members' dementia in hindsight—usually *after* getting a diagnosis. Before the diagnosis, they had grappled with symptoms, but like us, they didn't know what to do next.

The realization that Mom might have dementia compelled us to research this disease. We discovered a wealth of information online that should have come to our attention earlier, and guilt overwhelmed us. After noticing signs of dementia for months or years, guilt is a common response to discovering that a parent or spouse has the disease. Like others, we may have felt badly because we thought we *should* have recognized that Mom had dementia.

This is really where our story about advocacy begins. Once we knew something was wrong, we rallied together and intervened on Mom's behalf. We didn't understand the course of dementia for a long time, and our response was not always perfect. But could we have done better, knowing what we know now? We think so, and that is why we've written this book. We hope that our experiences will prompt other families to take action when they experience similar changes in a loved one's behavior.

Just imagine Mom's transformation as we pictured it. Born in Canada, Mom was touring in the United States during World War II and met her husband-to-be on a bus while he was on furlough. Mom became a war bride in short order. Not long after, the first of us arrived, and our family began life in a small Washington paper mill town. The rest of us followed as Dad's auto dealership prospered in the postwar economy.

We grew up in this small town in the fifties—the era of wringer washers, dial telephones, and the biggest event of our time, a black-and-white television. Our mother was a city girl at heart and railed against raising us in a rural home located three miles from town. In 1955, we moved into a new family home in the town proper. Mom remained there for eighteen years, until our father died in 1973.

Mom was a model housewife and embraced the expectations of her era. She cooked three meals a day from scratch, ironed, sewed beautiful clothing, and drove us to almost every activity available in the area: gymnastics, piano, swimming and dancing lessons, Girl Scout meetings, birthday parties, school plays, and concerts.

Education was important to her. She had dropped out of high school in the tenth grade but viewed it as a mistake. After marrying, she enrolled in a high-school completion program at a nearby community college and received her diploma. She read the daily newspaper religiously and watched the evening news, making herself aware of what was happening in her own community and around the world. After we left home, Mom was still cutting self-help articles from the newspaper and mailing little object lessons to us.

In later years, after the death of our father, Mom's artistic talent emerged, and she would paint prolifically for the next thirty years. She studied with regional and national artists, taking both local and out-of-town art classes. She won many ribbons in regional competitions for oil painting and watercolor. She also tried her hand at sculpture and gourd-making. Her artwork was displayed in the homes of family and friends.

Mom had a strong sense of adventure. After our father's death, she purchased a thirty-two-foot recreational vehicle, caravanned to Mexico with family members, and returned with stories about Los Angeles traffic that are now the stuff of family legend. She also travelled to Canada, the Philippines, England, and other countries by herself or with friends. Mom was extremely active in sports; she enjoyed downhill skiing in her fifties and laced up some new Rollerblades in her sixties for a spin around the block. She enjoyed walking, hiking, and bicycling. If you had suggested skydiving, she would have said, "Let's go!" She settled for parasailing in Hawaii.

Mom was at her best in the role of a family advocate. Relatives or friends who didn't have families of their own were included in holiday and birthday celebrations, and they were always invited to stay at our house if they were visiting from out of town. In later years, we followed this example and did the same for others.

Above all, Mom was fair-minded and insisted on justice. She was a consumer advocate early on. If a product she purchased was defective, letters of complaint were mailed off to the store or manufacturer. She was outspoken about what she felt was right and frequently spoke her mind to whoever she thought *could* make things right. From the model housewife of the fifties, Mom became the modern woman who reveled in free expression. She was no saint, though. She freely expressed herself, and her comments were often tinged with criticism, ranging from complaints about someone's choice of clothing to being served lukewarm coffee at restaurants.

The slow descent of someone like this into dementia is a difficult thing to watch. It is frustrating and emotionally defeating for the family, as well as for the dementia patient. The "person who was" would surface from time to time in the coming years, but would never return entirely.

What is Dementia?

A few years after our mother was diagnosed with dementia, we discovered that it is not a specific disorder or disease. Dementia is an umbrella term that covers many types of diseases. These diseases result in decreased memory, difficulties with thinking and reasoning, and decreased ability to care for oneself. Dementia is diagnosed when someone's functions are impaired in at least two of several areas: language and communication skills, ability to focus and pay attention, reasoning and judgment, visual perception, loss of memory, or problems with motor skills.[1]

It's important to note that some dementias are reversible. These dementias may result from depression, dietary deficiencies, or metabolic disorders.[2] This underlines the importance of getting a proper diagnosis, so that reversible forms can be ruled out. Unfortunately, many people find out that their dementia, like our mother's, is not reversible.

For these people, dementia is a progressive neurological condition that cannot be cured. As the disease progresses, the brain fails to function properly. This, in turn, affects all of the organs and systems controlled by the brain. Failure of these systems results in a variety of medical complications and considerably shortens a person's life-span.[3]

Although dementia is not caused by aging itself, it is quite common in older people. The prevalence of dementia increases rapidly with age, doubling every five years after age sixty. Dementia affects only 1 percent of people age sixty to sixty-four, but this number increases to 30–50 percent for those older than eighty-five.[4]

It's surprising, with odds like these, that people don't always visit their doctors when they experience symptoms of memory loss. What keeps them away? Changes may be so gradual that some people may simply not know they have a problem. But many experts believe that dementia patients are simply in denial. Patients may know they have a problem, but they deny it's dementia, because it might mean losing control of their lives. The problem is compounded by the fact that dementia is considered a mental illness by some professionals and businesses, and no one wants to be considered mentally ill.

Mark Kleinman, MD, a board-certified family physician, agrees. He says, "In my experience, the time from the patient's awareness of symptoms to diagnosis can be months or even years. The patient is in denial because of the stigma many people attach to dementia and other brain disorders."[5] No one wants to be labeled "crazy," so the dementia patient generally masks the problem and avoids getting a diagnosis. When a loved one exhibits signs of memory loss, denial may extend to family members as well.

In some cases, family and friends might know something is wrong, but they are reluctant to get involved. Sometimes they are apathetic about the situation, or they react with a "wait and see" approach to what is already developing into something serious. All of these attitudes complicate a looming problem. We spoke to some of Mom's friends after her death, who said they had noticed years earlier that Mom's behavior had been changing. Fearful of losing her car and her independence, Mom asked her friends not to discuss her difficulties with family members.

This secrecy confirms what Dr. Derick Scovel, a PhD in clinical psychology, says about dementia, "It can be perceived as a mental illness, with the social issues and stigma that go along with social and psychological problems. In truth, dementia is a neurological disease with very real and serious physical health consequences." Scovel's practice focuses on geriatric (elderly) patients with dementia. He says that most patients he sees are in denial about their condition on the first visit. Many family members ignore or dismiss the early signs of dementia and remain in denial until the signs are no longer mild. They often don't get a diagnosis until they are in a moderate stage, when crises begin to occur.[6]

Dismissing signs of early dementia can work at cross purposes. A good diagnosis can jump-start planning for the care and support that a person with dementia might need. The earlier dementia is diagnosed, the better the opportunity for treatment—and possible delay—of the progression of symptoms.[7]

Testing and Diagnosis for Dementia

Looking back now, it's interesting to note that Mom was the first person to have an idea that something was wrong. In 2005, she had been worried about memory loss for some time and had questioned her doctor about the possibility of Alzheimer's. The doctor's reassurance seemed false: "If you're aware enough to be worried about Alzheimer's, then you don't have it." Mom was reassured, but she pressed the matter again and asked if there were tests for Alzheimer's. Years later, we learned that her doctor had ordered lab and diagnostic tests at the time, but we weren't aware of further attempts by the doctor to explore Mom's concerns. We never heard about the outcome.

Her memory problems continued for several years after the initial inquiry into Alzheimer's, and finally she found a family-practice physician specializing in geriatrics. The doctor agreed to new diagnostic tests and referred Mom to a social worker for evaluation. By this time, we had caught on to the seriousness of Mom's condition and began going with her to her appointments. Having direct access to her doctor gave us an opportunity to ask questions of our own and confirm what she was telling us.

If a family suspects memory loss, early oversight of a person's medical care is critical, primarily to make sure that the doctor's instructions are followed. Imagine what it must be like for the person with dementia. First, there is the prospect of sorting out symptoms and figuring out their causes. Compound this with numerous doctor visits, test-taking, and inability to comprehend test results. Chances are, a loved one wouldn't understand or remember what she hears, making it difficult to participate in her treatment.

Coming to grips with dementia begins with a diagnosis, and a primary doctor is usually the starting point for this evaluation. The doctor will take a medical history and perform a physical exam to identify signs of other possible illnesses and side effects of medications that can mimic dementia. Lab and diagnostic tests can rule out treatable causes of increased confusion or memory loss.

The primary doctor may refer the patient to a neurologist to evaluate balance, sensory function, and reflexes, or to identify conditions that may affect the diagnosis or are treatable with medication. Today, neurologists can use tools like CT scans and magnetic resonance imaging (MRI) to have a look at the brain. These imaging technologies can uncover past strokes, tumors, or other problems that may cause dementia. Alzheimer's disease changes brain structure over time and is also visible with the aid of a brain scan. Scans can identify the effects of strokes or excess fluid on the brain.[8] Not all doctors recommend a CT or MRI, because imaging alone can't be used to diagnose dementia. But imaging can be useful in conjunction with lab results and other evaluations to create a more complete picture of what's occurring in the brain.

Dementia can also be unmasked through a variety of cognitive function tests administered by a social worker or psychologist. These tests are designed to measure a variety of skills and to evaluate memory, reasoning, and judgment. At this point, readers may be asking, "Why all these tests?" The goal is to determine whether dementia is present, its severity, and what part of the brain is affected.[9]

Two such memory tests are the Mini-Mental Status Exam (MMSE) and the St. Louis University Mental Status Exam (SLUMS). These tests and their purposes are described in more detail in appendix 1. A social worker usually administers and scores the tests. Memory tests do not provide a conclusive diagnosis for dementia and must be evaluated in conjunction with other tests.

Understanding Types of Dementia

There are many types of dementia, and people often ask why it's important to know what type someone has.

Dr. Scovel says, "it's not enough just to know you have dementia. It's a neurological disease with several forms. By way of comparison, an oncologist doesn't say, 'You have cancer. Come in for chemotherapy and I'll see you again in a month.' No, you'd want to know the type of cancer and identify what available treatment is best to treat the cancer for the best prognosis possible. You would want to know if the cancer treatment includes surgery, chemotherapy, drugs, radiation, and in what combination."[10]

Alzheimer's disease is often the first thing that springs to mind when we think of memory loss. The most common type of dementia, it accounts for an estimated 60–80 percent of cases. Hallmark abnormalities are deposits of plaques and twisted strands of the protein tau (tangles), as well as evidence of nerve cell damage and death in the brain.[11] But Alzheimer's disease isn't the only type of dementia. Other conditions can cause progressive changes in memory, communication, behavior, judgment, and the ability to function day-to-day.

Nearly forty different diseases and conditions can cause dementia, ranging from dietary deficiencies and metabolic disorders to head injuries and inherited diseases. Some of the more well-known causes of dementia are:

- *vascular dementia,* the second most common form of dementia, caused by poor blood flow to the brain;

- *mixed dementia,* dementia caused by more than one medical condition, most commonly both Alzheimer's and vascular disease;

- *dementia with Lewy bodies (DLB),* characterized by abnormal protein deposits called Lewy bodies, which appear in nerve cells in the brain stem;

- *frontotemporal dementia,* a rare disorder causing damage to brain cells in the frontal and temporal lobes. Pick's disease is the most common of the frontotemporal dementia types;

- *Creutzfeldt-Jacob dementia (CJD),* a degenerative neurological disorder, also known as mad cow disease;

- *normal pressure hydrocephalus (NPH),* involving an accumulation of cerebrospinal fluid in the brain's cavities;

- *Huntington's disease,* an inherited progressive dementia that affects cognition, behavior, and movement;

- *Parkinson's disease dementia (PDD),* a chronic, progressive neurological condition. Not all people with Parkinson's will develop dementia. This disease is also a Lewy body dementia.[12]

With so many different types of dementia, getting a proper diagnosis is important, particularly if there is a condition present that mimics the disease. Dementia, for example, may also be associated with depression, low levels of thyroid hormone, or deficiencies in niacin or vitamin B12. As mentioned earlier, dementia related to these conditions is often reversible.[13] Dr. Scovel, in fact, advises that "an advocate must be persistent (with the doctor) and say: 'I understand there are many kinds of dementia; each one has a different cause and prognosis, and each one is treated differently. I want to know what type of dementia this is.'"[14]

Such detailed information about dementia takes a while to digest. Our research, together with Mom's history of uncontrolled hypertension and small strokes, led us to conclude she probably had vascular dementia, but we never got a specific diagnosis. Having discovered this in hindsight, now we realize the importance of stepping in early and getting a diagnosis when a problem is first detected. Because we didn't, we were unaware that Mom was on a rapid slide downward, and that her life would come to a close much earlier than we had thought.

Stages of Dementia

"Stage" is simply a term that describes a group of behaviors and medical issues that tend to cluster together as dementia progresses. Some types of dementia can remain in the same stage for the rest of the person's life, depending on the cause. Head trauma is an example of this. All other dementias will progressively worsen. There are no clear definitions indicating when a stage starts or ends. Each person's experience is different; symptoms may change daily, or they may plateau for months at a time. However, as dementia progresses, some behaviors or medical issues gradually become less noticeable, while others move to the forefront. When this happens, it's important to take note, because the changes may signal a progression of the condition and a move to a new stage.[15]

Signs of physical and mental decline accompany these changes. Each person's experience will depend on many factors: the type of dementia, the age of onset, whether other illnesses are present, and what type of care the person receives. Each person's course of dementia is unique. What happens to one person won't necessarily happen to another.

Doctors traditionally divide the progression of dementia into three stages:

Stage 1   Mild or early stage of dementia
Stage 2   Moderate or middle stage of dementia
Stage 3   Severe or late stage of dementia

The stages overlap considerably, so you can't always categorize a person's symptoms easily. Scovel says, "The three-stage model may look different for various types of dementia." He suggests asking the family physician to explain the difference in stages as it applies to a family member's case, and asking what the family might expect to happen next. It could progressively get worse, but worse in a different way from other types of dementia.[16]

Stage 1: Mild or Early Stage of Dementia (Lasts Two to Four Years)

In this stage, loss of recent memory loss occurs frequently, particularly of recent conversations and events. The person will continually repeat the same questions and have some problems expressing and understanding language. There will be mild coordination problems; for instance, writing and using objects becomes difficult. Depression and apathy can occur, accompanied by mood swings. The person needs reminders for daily activities and may have difficulty driving.[17]

A person with mild dementia can live independently for the most part, taking care of things like bathing, house cleaning, and laundry. Judgment is relatively intact, but people may have problems dealing with tasks at work and participating in social activities.

Our own experience puts this group of symptoms for mild dementia in perspective. Mom was having difficulty living on her own, but we didn't appreciate what was really happening. Safety issues were first and foremost. Her driving, in our opinion, had never been good, but now it was downright risky. Occasionally, one of us would follow Mom home to check on her driving habits. Sometimes she veered into other lanes of traffic, and sometimes she drove slowly and then speeded up. She no longer signaled for turns. If we accompanied her to medical appointments or lunches, we insisted on driving.

Mom also had increasing difficulty with planning, reasoning, problem solving, and multitasking. "Executive function" is a term often used to describe these problems, and they often indicate signs of mild dementia.[18] Mom found it difficult to do things that used to be easy; she couldn't remember how to operate her CD player or turn on the radio. The television and VCR remotes stymied her. Each time we visited, Mom mentioned that she couldn't get her TV to work or told us she had "pushed the wrong buttons and now everything was messed up."

Mom loved to cook, but her frustration with following recipes from start to finish was evident. We might be able to read a list of ingredients ourselves, measure them, assemble them into a casserole, and bake them. For the person with dementia, the sheer number of steps and the planning required to execute them may seem overwhelming. We had to work alongside Mom, giving her a single task, like chopping onions, while we prepared and assembled the rest of the ingredients. Mom could spoon the ingredients into the casserole dish and level them out. We could open the oven door, and she could put the casserole in the oven.

These apparent problems with executive function also affected Mom's ability to do paperwork. She had long been a fan of Post-it notes, but now her kitchen counter and dining-room table were awash in a sea of tiny reminders. Invoices and donation requests marched in little columns across the dining room table. She didn't take action on them, however; she had lost her organizational skills.

We hadn't thought much about these changes at first. Many older people, including ourselves, have had similar age-related memory problems at times. In fact, it's very common to joke about forgetfulness as we age. But when someone has dementia, it's no longer a joke. If he or she is worried, *we* should take it seriously. Now we look back on the times we shrugged off Mom's concerns about Alzheimer's and reassured her everything was probably okay. She was reaching out. Her doctor didn't appreciate her concerns, and we didn't have enough information about dementia to recognize a problem.

In retrospect, had we understood the signs of early dementia, our response to Mom's difficulties would have been much different. First and foremost, we would have taken steps earlier to make sure she was in a safe environment. Her driving habits should have been addressed earlier, and we would have intervened sooner to help with bill paying, appointments, medication, and other activities requiring planning and organization. It's easy to look back and judge what *should* have been done when there is an understanding of what a diagnosis of dementia really means. Because we misunderstood the disease, we thought we could deal with Mom's difficulties by helping her "organize" her life.

Stage 2: Moderate or Middle Stage of Dementia
(Lasts Two to Ten Years)

It's difficult to tell when someone has crossed the line from mild to moderate dementia, because changes may take place gradually over a period of years. In the moderate stage, a person can no longer cover up the problems she is having. There is pervasive and persistent memory loss, including forgetfulness about personal history and inability to recognize friends and family. She has rambling speech, unusual reasoning, and confusion about current events, time, and place. She is more likely to become lost in familiar settings, experience sleep disturbances, and have changes in mood and behavior, which can be aggravated by stress and change. She may experience delusions, aggression, and uninhibited behavior. Mobility and coordination is affected by slowness, rigidity, and tremors. She needs structure, reminders, and assistance with the activities of daily living.[19]

Communication is often a problem in the moderate stage of dementia. Over time, Mom's ability to carry on a conversation dwindled. For most people, conversation is a back-and-forth discussion of ideas. Each person picks up on the other's thought and adds his own, and the exchange can go on for several minutes. As Mom's dementia progressed into the middle stage, she lost the ability to converse and could only respond to one question at a time with a short sentence. She simply wasn't able to pick up on a thought and move the conversation forward. At some level, Mom *wanted* to have a conversation, so she repeated exactly whatever we said, as if she had just come up with the idea on her own.

Mom often lost track of time. She didn't know the time of day and couldn't use the clock as a reminder to go to activities. She missed a lot because of this. After she moved into a care facility, mealtimes were a problem. If she didn't get a reminder from facility staff, she would forget to eat altogether. Sometimes she forgot she had just eaten an hour earlier, wondered why the dining room wasn't open, and demanded to eat.

Mom's short-term memory loss was frustrating for us, and we learned new lessons in tolerance. At one assisted living facility, she purchased swimsuits at a nearby shopping mall over and over again, forgetting that her dresser was filled with them. She lost her sense of modesty and tried to go into the pool without a swimsuit. Problems with getting dressed took on new proportions. Often we'd arrive at the facility to find Mom ready for a swim—underwear under her swimsuit and street clothes over it, with a purple house dress on top of everything else. We donned our own swimsuits, got into the pool with her, and guided her through the water aerobics class routine. Afterward, we helped her shower and dress, because she couldn't do it alone.

Mom had been an artist for three decades. When she moved to assisted living, she gradually lost interest in painting. In earlier years in her own home, several projects would be going at once, but now she couldn't select materials or organize even one project. She could still paint if water, brushes, and paint were placed in front of her. As her dementia advanced, she completely lost interest in painting.

Confusion and incidents of memory loss prompted us to keep a closer watch on her activities after she moved to assisted living. We started taking turns visiting Mom three days a week. After the visits, we wrote e-mails to update the others about Mom's medical condition and her response to activities. At the time, we didn't know that these reports would blossom into more than twenty-five hundred e-mails over a period of five years. We shared many humorous occasions in these writings, but many more were sad accounts of Mom's decline. Most importantly, the e-mails recorded our impressions of Mom's changes in judgment and behavior over time.

In the moderate stage of dementia, people benefit from more structure and supervision. Someone must be available to tell them exactly what to do or what will happen next. Although they can do many things by themselves, they may need prompting to get started. In our mother's memory care facility, we frequently noticed caregivers reassuring people with detailed descriptions of what was to happen next. "Now I'm going to take your arm and help you stand up. Then we're going to walk." This verbal inventory of upcoming events dampens the anxiety of not knowing what's to come.

The need for more assistance with meals, using the bathroom, dressing, and other personal activities is characteristic in this phase of dementia. The amount of assistance a person needs varies. Mom, for example, was able to eat and use the bathroom on her own for quite some time, but she had problems choosing what to wear and getting dressed. She dressed herself in unusual ways—six socks on one foot, two on the other. When she couldn't decide what else to put on, she might resort to a wardrobe of bra and slacks until a caregiver caught up with her and dressed her appropriately. She would look at her cosmetics and say, "I don't know what to do with these things." Every morning, a caregiver would lay out an outfit for Mom to wear and set out shoes on the floor near her bed. Sometimes the caregiver would have to peel off several layers of socks before her shoes would fit.

Stage 3: Severe or Late Stage of Dementia (Lasts One to Three-Plus Years)

In this stage, the person with dementia is confused about past and present. She loses the ability to remember, communicate, or process information. Verbal skills may be lost entirely. People in this stage of dementia cannot care for themselves, and a variety of physical problems may emerge. A person might fall more easily or have trouble bending arms and legs or walking. Problems with swallowing and incontinence may occur. Problems with mood, behavior, hallucinations, and delirium may become extreme. In this stage, the person needs around-the-clock, intensive support and care.[20]

Illnesses that would be minor for a younger person can affect a person with dementia more dramatically. When Mom had a urinary tract infection, for example, her behavior was distinctly different from her "normal" dementia behavior. She was more disoriented than usual and appeared weak and frail. The disorientation quickly disappeared after Mom took antibiotics, and she came back to life.

Mom's decrease in mobility was more evident as she entered the final stage of dementia. Her arms became rigid, and her fingers gradually curled into fists. Because she couldn't open her hands, she couldn't grasp the bars of her walker, which increased her risk of falling. Mom's ability to walk also declined dramatically during the last few months of her life. In the moderate stage of dementia, she had been able to walk without assistance. Now she could no longer walk independently and turned to a walker. During the last six months of her life, she fell several times and was finally confined to a wheelchair.

Eating seems like such a natural function of life that we take it for granted. But the ability to eat solid foods may be lost with advanced dementia. Swallowing became a problem for Mom, and she began choking during meals. When she could no longer eat solid food, her diet transitioned to purees of items from the dining room's daily menu. It was common to visit her at mealtime and see pureed short ribs and blended pasta salad in custard cups sitting before her.

People unfamiliar with caring for advanced dementia patients might not be aware of how hard it is to drink liquids. We learned that thickeners were available to reduce problems with choking. It was a surprise to learn that even water, coffee, and fruit juice could be thickened to make drinking easier.

Mom's eating and drinking problems were accompanied by general physical decline. Now she needed help to eat, bathe, dress, and do everything else a person would normally be able to do without assistance. Mom wasn't able to recognize pictures of family and friends in her photo albums, and she no longer recognized her own artwork on the walls in her apartment. From her reaction when we entered a room, we were pretty certain she recognized us on most days. Her face lit up, and a smile crossed her face. Some days, however, were different; Mom would be staring into space when we arrived and wouldn't react at all.

A better understanding of dementia might have helped us cope with these developments. During the mild stage of the disease, we expected that Mom would gradually lose her mental capability, but we did not expect the physical problems that would accompany her decline. As time went on, we were dismayed to see her physical abilities spiraling downward.

The emotional impact of dementia on families is considerable. If we'd understood the progress of dementia beforehand, it would have tempered our reactions to Mom's changing physical and mental abilities. We could have anticipated what kind of help Mom might need. Most important, we would have stepped in sooner to help. We concluded that a solid understanding of the progress of dementia is essential.

At the time Mom started having problems, our pathway to getting a diagnosis and treatment was rocky at best. Our confusion about how to handle the changes she was experiencing was central to the problem. Now we know that medications are available to help control symptoms of dementia. Their ability to help varies for each person, and their effectiveness depends on specific symptoms and on the stage of dementia. Some medications can slow the progression of dementia in the early stages, although they may only work for certain types of dementia and not for others.

Perhaps one of the biggest arguments for understanding the three stages of dementia is that an awareness of what's to come can help the family plan in advance. If we had known Mom was in the early stage of dementia, we would have reached out to her in different ways. A discussion about her ideas for end-of-life medical care would have helped with decisions that we faced later. She may have had different preferences about her personal and spiritual care that we could have addressed.

Our initial lack of awareness about the stages of dementia had a direct impact on the difficulties Mom experienced in assisted living. At the time, our goal was to give her the most independence possible with minimal supervision. In reality, Mom was already in the moderate (or second) stage of dementia and wandering away from the facility without a companion had put her safety at risk.

Mom's strong will and drive for independence were single-minded. These characteristics had a lot to do with her conflicts with staff in assisted living. She liked going out of the building for coffee, but then she'd get lost. Attempts at persuading her to stay, or redirecting her, didn't usually succeed. Staff frequently argued with her, which made no difference to Mom. She was not inclined to listen to anyone. We tried to placate her each time problems arose by keeping her busy and away from staff. In reality, we couldn't see the big picture. Had we understood her behavior in the context of the disease's progress, we might have moved her to a locked memory-care facility much sooner.

Treatment Plans for Dementia

In retrospect, a treatment plan would have benefitted the entire family. What do we mean by a treatment plan? Suppose someone has been diagnosed with high blood pressure. Her doctor would prescribe a course of action that might include medication to lower blood pressure, a "prescription" for exercise, an improved diet, and regular monitoring to make sure blood pressure is under control. These measures, taken together, form a treatment plan for high blood pressure. Meanwhile, a person could research the causes and effects of high blood pressure and learn additional ways to control it.

A treatment plan for dementia works much the same way. Because dementia is a progressive disease, the course of treatment will change as physical and mental abilities decline. Once the physician or psychologist diagnoses the type and stage of dementia, a plan can be tailored to a person's individual needs. Each plan should include follow-up medical care at regular intervals to monitor progress. Medications approved for dementia may be prescribed to slow the progression of the disease and improve mental function, mood, or behavior.

Treatment plans are about more than just medications. If a family member is diagnosed with mild dementia, she may still be capable of participating in decision making about her care. The treatment plan for this stage may include ways to support independent living by helping with management of daily tasks. Support groups offer information on the impact of the disease and how to cope with it, and they can help family advocates, as well as the person with dementia. When someone has mild dementia, it is the time to make plans for the future—preparing advance care plans, estate planning, and determining future wishes about home care or care in a facility.

Because balance and mobility decline with moderate dementia, more intensive help and close supervision are needed to prevent falling. Different medications might be needed for anxiety, depression, or agitation. The physical environment must be modified to accommodate changing needs. For example, area rugs must be removed to prevent tripping, a walk-in shower with a stool might be needed for safety, and more assistance with bathing, dressing, and other needs may be required. Support-group meetings help the family cope with the sense of loss they experience as a loved one gradually declines. In this sense, the treatment plan is expanded to include the entire family.

In advanced dementia, basic activities such as eating, dressing, bathing, using the bathroom, and simply moving around become more difficult or impossible for someone to do alone. Intensive medical interventions do not prolong life, so facilities and families can step in with comfort measures. Treatment plans are flexible and can be modified to take these needs into account.

If we had understood the stages of dementia, we would have had a better idea about the best treatment plan for Mom. Dr. Derick Scovel, the clinical psychologist quoted earlier, adds this about treatment plans: "There are general overviews of treatment based on the type of dementia. But sometimes, the family doesn't want to try something that's recommended, or the patient has a bad reaction to a medication. It involves a lot of trial and error. A good treatment plan starts with general guidelines, which are usually based on research and evidence. Follow-up is necessary to find out what works, so treatment plans need to be tailored to family decisions and the patient's response to the interventions. "The family advocate needs to tell the doctor what's working and what's not working. Everyone has to work as a team. The psychologist's responsibility is to establish rapport with the patient and family. The psychologist also must communicate his recommendations to the family physician, who needs to have an overall view of the situation. A bad family advocate is a giant speed bump. He is not open to conflicting ideas and won't work cohesively in a team. In a good team, everyone's talking and in agreement about what works."

Scovel adds that a patient has a better quality of life if the family and health-care providers are working as a team. As a result, families don't feel like they're always flying by the seat of their pants. "All the arrangements can seem to be working perfectly until the patient transitions to a new stage," Scovel says, "but at least you have some idea about what can happen next."[21]

Scovel's advice about treatment plans seems to make sense. Looking back on the course of Mom's dementia, we wish we'd known about treatment plans from the beginning. Dementia, like most other diseases that occur during the course of our lives, should have a treatment plan. Scovel drives this point home in a neat summary. "There are no silver bullets. You've got to think silver *buckshot*," he says. "The best treatment plan for a dementia or Alzheimer's patient combines a variety of approaches: the right medications, the right environment for that particular patient's needs and stage of dementia, and the support of advocates who understand the disease, can anticipate stages and know what to expect."[22]

Looking back, we can understand the advantages of treatment plans. For the patient, they offer the best quality of care for her needs. For the family, they are guidelines that remove uncertainty from daily decisions and help put these decisions in context. Our advice to other families is to meet with family doctors, ask about treatment plans, and determine a course of action. Investigate resources that might be available to fund these plans and to provide the types of assistance needed.

A psychologist who regularly works with geriatric patients can conduct verbal testing. He can meet with the family and the dementia patient to determine family history, identify the type of dementia, make a prognosis, and prepare a treatment plan. A cooperative approach in this evaluation ensures that everyone is on the same page.

Lessons Learned

- If a spouse or loved one is experiencing memory problems, listen to the inner voice that indicates something might be wrong. We should have taken Mom to a doctor or a psychologist with geriatric experience when she first expressed concerns about memory loss.

- When Mom first started having problems, we didn't know about the importance of getting a dementia diagnosis or developing a treatment plan. Now we know that a good advocate does research in advance, knows what to ask for, and has well-informed questions for the doctor.

- We should have attended an Alzheimer's support group to learn from other family members about coping with dementia. As a family of four sisters, we assumed we could understand dementia by discussing Mom's behaviors and physical problems with each other. After Mom's death, we attended a support group to find out what we missed. We discovered we had lost out on a wealth of information from other families about what to expect and how to handle our own emotional reactions.

- We could have talked more with Mom's doctors about medications that might have helped with memory loss, physical problems, or agitation in the various stages of dementia. This knowledge would have tempered our response to drugs we assumed were used just to calm people with dementia.

- Most of all, we hadn't understood the end result of this disease. We assumed it would go on for years as someone aged naturally. Dementia is not a mental problem. It is a disease in its own right, and it is terminal. A lot of information is available about dementia. We wish we'd paid more attention to newspaper, magazine, and Internet articles about the disease. This would have been useful early on in identifying the signs, types, and stages of dementia.

- In talking with colleagues and other people in our own circles of friends, we realized that few families recognize symptoms or understand treatments and appropriate living situations for a family member with dementia. For anyone who suspects a family member might have dementia, our message is see the primary care doctor and get on the road to a diagnosis, if indicated.

CHAPTER TWO

CARE FACILITIES: MAKING
THE RIGHT MOVE

As the summer of 2005 reached its peak, Mom was still firmly entrenched in her small ranch house on Arizona Drive. She could manage on her own, she thought, but the reality was different. Our visits weren't just social anymore. We mowed the lawn, raked the leaves, and did the heavy lifting to prevent another accident. Months before, Mom had tugged an overloaded leaf bin across the yard and hurt her back when it fell on her.

She didn't seem to be aware that outside chores were too difficult. Her independent streak overshadowed her ability to set limits, and we had to work hard to overcome her resistance to accepting help. With increasing confusion and decreasing judgment, she wasn't realistic about her physical capabilities.

It would be two years before we learned enough about dementia to view her present difficulties in the long-term context of the disease. Had we known about stages of dementia and treatment plans earlier, it would have been easier to work with the changes Mom was experiencing.

In our opinion, living alone was no longer a safe option, and we discussed the idea of having her live with each of us for several months at a time. But Mom wasn't open to this idea. She also refused to have someone live with her at Arizona Drive, and we were at an impasse. Had we understood the steep cognitive declines that often accompany changes in location, we would not have considered moving rotations at all.

Friends and relatives had faced similar decisions with aging parents, and we turned to them for advice. Some parents had moved in with adult children, other families had opted for full-time care in the parents' homes. Still other parents had moved into care facilities. Some had physical disabilities, others had Alzheimer's or dementia. Some parents had both. We decided that care facilities were Mom's best option, and we made appointments to visit several in the surrounding community.

We'd always thought that all care facilities were nursing homes, places where older people lived while they were waiting to die. This simplistic view was uninformed at best, and it was hard to put our prejudices aside. Later we would learn that care facilities are active social communities with unique cultures of their own.

The world of long-term care facilities is not simple, but we never imagined the array of living arrangements and types of services that were available. Care facilities aren't just places to live, they are places that must follow a bewildering set of rules that dictate family choices in living arrangements. Care facilities are governed by state licenses that regulate the types of services they can provide.

At first we weren't aware of the restrictions. We thought Mom could live anywhere we chose, and we struck out blindly, looking at anything and everything. One friend recommended an adult family home, which prompted us to look at several in the area. We opened the phone book and found other types of facilities. As we visited each place, we measured Mom's strong personality against each potential living situation and graded it by how she might accept living there. But like it or not, it wasn't really our choice. If the facility wasn't licensed to provide the services Mom needed, she couldn't move in.

Mom's medication errors were the biggest issue. She needed supervision: a service available in assisted living or memory care. When we finally found a facility that Mom liked, only one independent living apartment was available, in an area of the facility not licensed to manage medications. The timing was right for Mom's move, so we finessed a care situation that fell between two different regulatory settings. As an interim solution, we hired a private licensed practical nurse (LPN) to give Mom her medications until an assisted living apartment became available.

Types of Care Facilities

Many types of care facilities are available across the United States, and the range of choices increases the likelihood of finding a successful match. It's smart for families to consider all of the options, especially when a loved one has physical problems along with dementia. Specialized living situations are available for everyone who needs care outside of a private home.

When we began our search, we didn't have a clear understanding of the differences among facilities, and we learned about their services and restrictions as we went along. For those just beginning, it's helpful to start with a look at the general categories of facilities.

Continuing Care Retirement Communities (CCRCs)

These communities offer an entire spectrum of care services, including all of the services mentioned in the paragraphs below. Their multiple state licenses define services that can be offered in each area of their facilities. Residents may transfer from one area of a CCRC to another as needs change, keeping within the facility's licensing mandates. CCRCs generally require large, upfront buy-ins. An ownership interest in a CCRC will guarantee a lifetime residence, as long as residents make the required monthly payments. CCRCs are also known as life estate communities.

Independent Living

These facilities offer private rental apartments. Recreational facilities such as gyms or swimming pools may be available. Apartments are usually equipped with pull cords for emergencies, but independent living facilities cannot help people directly; they are required to call 911. Independent apartments may include cleaning services and meal plans in a common dining area. Apartments are usually equipped with kitchens and sometimes private laundry hookups. A variety of social programs such as field trips and entertainment are included in the pricing. Residents who need help with the activities of daily living (ADLs: bathing, dressing, help with eating, and so forth) must arrange for these services privately. Facility employees are not licensed to help independent living residents.

Assisted Living

These facilities offer help with ADLs. Levels of care may vary from one facility to another, a factor that plays into the long-term choices a family makes. Families should look for facilities that have a wide range of services that allow residents to remain in one place as long as possible.

Assisted living facilities generally offer all meals, apartment cleaning services, and optional help with laundry. Apartment pricing may include transportation to medical appointments, grocery stores, and shopping malls. Emergency pull cords are often located in bathrooms and bedrooms of assisted living apartments, and facility staff will personally respond to emergencies.

Adult Family Homes

These homes are licensed by states to care for a small number of people in a residential setting. They perform a full spectrum of care services and their monthly rates are often lower than other types of care facilities. Adult family homes have smaller staffs, so it is important to find out how their time is divided between physical care and social activities. If routine medical procedures are an issue, get specifics on how they are handled. Adult family homes may not be staffed with nurses or other medical professionals.

Skilled Nursing Facilities (SNFs)

Also called nursing homes, these facilities offer patients the highest level of medical care available outside of hospitals. All levels of long-term care are available, including care for people who are ambulatory (walking) and those who need more comprehensive care. SNFs also provide temporary, rehabilitative care (for example, recovery from surgery or a broken bone) that cannot be handled at home. They offer meals and all levels of group and in-room activities geared to residents' interests.

Alzheimer's and Memory Care Facilities

Services may be offered within a facility that is licensed for independent or assisted living or in a separate facility devoted to Alzheimer's and memory care. Most memory care residents will eventually need full assistance with the activities of daily living. Social and exercise programs help people retain memory skills as long as possible. Memory care facilities typically provide full dining, cleaning, and laundry services for residents. Many of these facilities are walled or fenced to prevent residents from wandering away.

The "Assisted Living State Regulatory Review 2012" standardizes a list of services that are available in care facilities in each state.[1] Descriptions are based on each state's regulations.

Guidelines for Screening Care Facilities

Loved ones will receive the best care if there is an effective partnership between the family and the care facility.

Before families begin the search, we recommend that they organize a plan for dividing care responsibilities among themselves. For example, who will make regular social visits, and who will be in charge of ensuring that a loved one is involved in outings and social activities? Who will be in charge of medical appointments and coordinating medical needs with the facility? Who will be the main family contact for the care facility? Should more than one family member be in charge of care decisions or should one person be in charge?

In the end, the facility has the primary responsibility for someone's care, so it's imperative that the facility meet all of a loved one's care needs. We recommend taking a checklist of requirements on facility visits and asking how the facility can meet each of them. Is there a medical issue that needs daily attention? Is there access to specific social activities like music or art? A checklist is a useful guideline for talking with staff and determining whether the facility will be a successful match.

Successful facility living depends on a loved one's ability to adapt to the daily routines. If memory loss is an issue, it's important to look at how routines will work in practice. Will a loved one spend time alone in her apartment unless invited to come out for social activities? Does she need reminders to come to meals? Will she be safe in an apartment without constant supervision? Is she highly mobile, and will she try to leave the facility on her own?

Placement success depends on a loved one's acceptance and enjoyment of activities and amenities. When prescreening facilities, ask for a copy of the monthly social calendar and talk with the activities director. A good activities director will organize quality social programs that involve residents at all stages of dementia. Before making a decision, take a loved one to a few activities at the facility to test the waters. Some facilities offer trial residence periods without contractual commitments. Some offer adult day care. Taking advantage of these services can help families decide whether a facility will work before signing a written agreement.

Before visiting facilities, contact state regulatory agencies responsible for overseeing their activities.[2] An excellent YouTube video describes a step-by-step process for looking up inspection reports on assisted living facilities.[3] Prescreening facilities will help keep the visits objective and develop interview questions about past inspections or violations. It's important to learn how facilities responded to past issues raised by state inspectors. Contact the state long-term care ombudsman's office for valuable information on criteria for selecting facilities.[4]

If the family has never visited a memory care facility, ask staff for a description of what the family will see before taking a tour. First-time visitors may be unprepared for residents' unexpected actions or behaviors and should be aware that it's "the dementia talking," not the people who have the disease. Upfront explanations prepare families to avoid the distractions of unfamiliar behavior.[5]

Facilities should be measured by the benefits they can offer to a family member. Focus on the services and activities and cleanliness of the environment and the residents. Note the attitude of the staff as they go about their work and observe whether they are talking *with* residents rather than *at* them.

Look beyond the décor, the dining room, and the facility's description of activities. Ask about resident-to-staff ratios and compare ratios among a number of facilities. In an industry where employee turnover rates are often high, staffing differences may result in differences in the quality of care.

If an Alzheimer's/memory care facility has an organized support group for families, ask for contact information. Before signing a residence agreement, attend a meeting and get the group's opinion about the facility. Strike up conversations with other residents or their families during facility visits. Ask to observe group activities. Drop in unannounced and get opinions from residents or their family members about what they like and don't like.

People with memory problems benefit from stable routines, but if they become ill and the facility cannot provide care because of state restrictions or internal policies, they may be forced to move. Some facilities are more flexible than others about handling temporary medical problems. A facility's policy on temporary illnesses may affect a loved one's long-term stay and the family's view on which facility to choose. If a loved one has special medical needs, set up an interview with the nursing staff to discuss how they will be handled.

Ask about billing practices and history of price increases. This will help determine whether prices fit within the family's budget. Although we wanted to move quickly, we took time to ask questions about costs and develop a long-term care budget. Chapter 3 talks about our strategy for determining costs and making adjustments in our budget as costs changed.

Ask which legal documents the facility requires for residence. These documents may include a living will, medical power of attorney (POA), and signed doctor's orders for end-of-life treatment (do not resuscitate or DNR order). Legal documents are usually referenced in residence agreements, and if they're not available, there may be delays in finalizing the agreement and moving in.

Hospice and palliative care services are another topic to consider when previewing care facilities. A facility's ability to provide quality end-of-life care is an important upfront consideration in choosing a facility. Asking about these services seemed untimely to us, because the idea of Mom's death was so remote. Staff will not usually mention end-of-life care arrangements during initial interviews, because they know that families are not prepared to hear this information.

It's up to families to initiate the conversation about end of life. Getting information before it's needed will help families prepare for a loved one's final days. If the facility doesn't offer hospice or palliative care services, a loved one may have to move just at the moment when familiar surroundings are needed. If hospice care can be provided at the facility, ask for recommendations about community hospice organizations and get familiar with their admission requirements.

Making the Choice: Our Concerns in Selecting a Care Facility

Mom wanted to be actively involved in the search for her new home, and this seemed reasonable, because she was in the early stage of dementia. But she was prone to snap judgments, so we decided to prescreen facilities before taking her on visits. We understood her tendency to reject new ideas, so our scouting tours ruled out choices she would find unacceptable. The tours also helped us guide her choices. Prescreening the facilities gave us talking points about the advantages of each facility when we returned for tours with Mom.

We previewed assisted living and memory care facilities and adult family homes. Tours were undertaken with an eye toward matching Mom's strong personality and active lifestyle to each living situation. Adult family homes were plentiful, and they promised home-like living environments. The ambience varied. Some were light and cheery, some dark and dreary. Most had tiny bedrooms, meeting the state's mandate[6] of an eighty-eight-square-foot minimum per person—barely room for a single bed, a small dresser, and a chair. Rooms were often home to oxygen tanks, walkers, and assistive lifts, reducing floor space even more.

Most adult family homes we previewed had double rooms with a shared bath—a clear lack of privacy. For someone accustomed to a solitary lifestyle, sharing a room didn't seem like a formula for success. Limited recreational activities were another drawback. In the homes we visited, since most residents were limited in mobility, days were typically confined to watching television, reading, listening to music, or visiting with family. Mom was physically active, and these homes didn't seem to match her current needs and interests.

We toured an Alzheimer's home on a large fenced lot. Like other adult family care facilities, the home was focused on meeting the day-to-day physical and medical needs of its residents. Social needs were considered extras. A separate monthly fee provided assistance with reading, crossword puzzles, or other one-on-one activities. Mom was functioning at a higher cognitive level than most of the residents, so this home wasn't a match. Now we were getting discouraged.

At this point, readers might be asking themselves if we'd lost sight of the goal. Our search devolved into arguments, and we were in deep disagreement about what to do next. These sisterly disagreements were the starting point for a lot of emotional ups and downs over the next few years. Acknowledging that a loved one has dementia and dealing with the day-to-day reality is stressful. Arguments compounded the difficulty of finding the right place for Mom, but we finally learned to set our personal feelings aside and make decisions objectively.

We learned that it's helpful for family members to acknowledge their differences in advance and to plan ways to settle them. Families should also discuss ways of helping each other deal with emotional needs, especially if one person is carrying more responsibility for care than the others. This may not seem important initially, but it becomes evident as caring for someone with dementia grows more challenging. We wish we had gone to Alzheimer's support-group meetings to learn more about these issues.

Halfway through our facility previews, we were introduced to a trained specialist who helped us narrow down facility choices. She interviewed our family and recommended concentrating our search on assisted living facilities, which would meet most of Mom's needs. Happily, the facility we chose would pay the specialist's commission, so for us her services were free.[7]

Meals and Menus in Care Facilities

Based on the specialist's recommendations, we made in-person visits to assisted living facilities and checked out atmosphere, services, and food. Apartments were equipped with stoves and microwaves (a safety risk for Mom), but if she liked the dining room's menu she would be less inclined to cook in her apartment. We learned that the staff unplugged stoves as a safety precaution when residents weren't able to use them safely.

Care facilities publish monthly menus, allowing families to preview the types of meals that are available. Many facilities have daily specials, ordered by many residents who have trouble making choices. When we set up appointments to visit facilities, sales staff invited us for lunch, allowing us to sample the food quality. Families can also make unannounced visits to facility dining rooms during meals to evaluate the flow of service and appearance of the food.

Residents can request standing orders for foods that they like (salads, for example). If they are restricted from eating certain foods because of medications or allergies, these restrictions are noted in the resident's chart, and the kitchen is informed. After a dining routine is established, it pays to make sure that kitchen staff and servers are aware of restrictions. Staff turnover is high, and servers often rotate among different jobs throughout the facility. Information about diet restrictions is not always communicated to the kitchen staff.

Social Activities in Care Facilities: What's Available to Keep People Interested?

A good activities director is the key to keeping things interesting for residents. We advise families to compare activity programs at several facilities to find things of interest to a loved one. Most of the assisted living facilities we previewed had ambitious social calendars, including weekly bus trips to grocery stores, shopping malls, garden centers, and scenic points of interest.

Gardening groups, card games, musical presentations, and wine socials kept residents busy into the early evening hours at many of the facilities we visited. Art classes were offered, too. Exercise classes, gyms, and swimming pools are among amenities in many assisted living facilities.

A few preliminary visits to a facility may uncover activities or programs that capture a family member's interest. Something like an art or history class may inspire a loved one's interest and ease her transition into a new setting. Matching interests is most successful when a facility offers social programs appropriate for different skill levels and cognitive abilities.

It's crucial to match the tone or *culture* of a facility to a family member's personality. If she is quiet or withdrawn, look for an environment that isn't noisy and filled with constant activity. If she is outgoing, find a facility where residents are highly engaged in social activities. Moving to a new place is an emotional experience for elders who aren't accustomed to change, and a good match will improve the chances of success.

After selling her home, Mom moved into an assisted living facility on a quiet street three blocks from a large shopping complex. The shopping mall was her idea of the perfect way to spend the day alone—shopping, drinking coffee, and people watching. Aside from a few art classes, Mom had never joined groups, and it was clear her ideas about social life at the new facility would be very different from ours.

We had expected her to embrace the facility's social programs, meet new people, and get involved. But Mom was slow to warm to the facility's activities, and she continued old patterns of shopping at the mall and lunching in restaurants with friends. We had been so caught up in the idea of moving that we hadn't paused to consider the consequences. This outcome underscores the importance of considering existing routines and interests when choosing a new place to live. A lifetime of habits doesn't change overnight.

Moving to a Care Facility: Dementia and Disorientation

Mom's memory problems increased dramatically after she moved. After thirty years of stable routines in the same household, her life was disrupted. Long afterward, we learned that when someone has dementia, sudden cognitive decline often accompanies a move to a new location. People may have trouble settling into new routines and seem lost, even though the new setting is filled with familiar furniture, clothing, and artwork.

We didn't realize that Mom's memories were solidly organized around *place*. When she lived at home, she knew where everything was, and now she couldn't find dishes, clothing, books, or toiletries. Her patterns of daily living had been uprooted, and the move had scrambled her cognitive map, adding to her confusion. Her belongings had come with her, but they were reassembled in a complicated new living arrangement.

During the move, we took the lead in organizing Mom's furniture, drawers, and cupboards in the new apartment, clearly a mistake. Mom kept offering us little clues to her distress. If she didn't know where things were, how could she find them when we weren't there? Thinking back, we realize Mom should have been allowed to believe she was in charge of unpacking and deciding where everything should be stored. She was at her calmest when in control of a situation.

Mom's judgment and reasoning ability were changing, and other problems surfaced after the move. Her safety, already at risk, made ordinary activities like taking walks and driving her car more dangerous. Mom had been silent about her driving problems, so we didn't know she had been getting lost, or losing her car in grocery store parking lots. Her fingers remained tightly wrapped around the keys to her Honda, until she left her car at a friend's condo and forgot where it was. The keys' mysterious disappearance after that incident led to rounds of anger and protest.[8]

Dementia and Wandering Outside a Care Facility: A Choice of Safety or Independence.

By car or on foot, assisted living facilities must allow people to come and go as they please. Mom took full advantage of this policy and left the facility frequently for walks. Memory problems continued to chip away at the safety of these outings, and she was routinely getting lost. If she asked for directions, she may not have understood them. Sometimes she even accepted rides from strangers. We pressed Mom to reconsider recreational and social activities inside the building and to stop going out.

In the months to come, the facility receptionist warned us that Mom was leaving the building more often. She couldn't remember to sign in and out at the front desk, a procedure that ensured everyone had returned safely. She took a bus to the library and got lost, and she tried to use a credit card to check out books. Mom returned to the facility twice in the tow of police, increasing our level of concern. One day she was discovered standing in the middle of a quiet street a block from the facility. That was the final warning bell.

Assisted living had seemed like a good transition from home. But almost a year had passed since she had moved, and we concluded that Mom's safety was still at risk. If she stayed in assisted living, she would continue living her life as she had at home, ignoring the facility and spending most of her time outside the building. We weren't ready to give up on assisted living, so we decided to try a different approach.

Switching Assisted Living Facilities: Making Sure It's the Right Move

We were at a crossroads, and our youngest sister, a nurse, proposed an adult family home or a locked memory care facility. Everyone else in the family disagreed. Emotions peaked as we argued about the next step. It seemed that our differences were more important than what was best for Mom. Our next decision, to move Mom to a facility that was miles from the shopping mall, was decidedly naïve. We had incorrectly assumed a change in location would take her mind off shopping, and she would forget about outside excursions.

A few visits to the new facility familiarized Mom with her new surroundings. Several in-laws and acquaintances lived there, so an instant social network was in place. We talked to Mom about the advantages of living near family, and we attended the facility's group activities with other family members. It appeared that the new situation might work. But once again we had underestimated the strength of old habits. Mom's behavior wasn't going to change, no matter where she lived. She stubbornly refused help and plowed ahead with her own agenda, seemingly unaware of safety consequences. Her judgment was on a downward spiral, and her behavior was as reckless as ever.

The new facility offered several levels of care, including a separate, unlocked memory care wing that opened into an assisted living complex. Mom moved into a sunny studio in memory care, which she found unsuitable almost immediately. It didn't take long to discover that Mom's social, physical, and mental abilities were better matched to the assisted living group in the main part of the complex.

Problems erupted shortly after the last piece of art-work was hung on her wall. Mom demanded to eat in the assisted living dining room. Memory care residents rarely talked, and many needed help with eating. Mom wasn't "one of those people." Tirades about living in memory care played out daily in front of the nurse's office, spurring a transfer to the assisted living section within a few weeks of the move.

Conflicts with Assisted Living Staff

During Mom's five years in care facilities, we spoke with residents who accepted their new accommodations and didn't push the boundaries. Many would have preferred to live in their own homes, but they understood why they couldn't. Some didn't like assisted living but decided to make the best of it. Others were satisfied, happy, and involved.

Not every person who moves to a care facility will have conflicts with staff, but our mother certainly did. She was single-minded and went up against staff members regularly. Our efforts to engage her in the facility's social programs were aimed at finding a positive outlet for her anger. We ramped up visiting schedules and accompanied Mom to water aerobics classes, movies, and in-house musical presentations. We hired an outside caregiver to help Mom with activities on days we couldn't visit. She gave up swimming on those days; the caregiver didn't swim, and Mom wasn't allowed in the pool without a companion. In fact, Mom relied heavily on companionship to guide her through daily activities, illustrating her decline in cognitive skills. Our visits were so frequent that we failed to notice this at first.

Near the end of Mom's stay in assisted living, her cognitive problems became more evident. She had little problem starting an activity on impulse, but she couldn't organize its parts once she got started. If she wanted to go swimming, it didn't matter whether the pool was open or whether her water aerobics class was in session. It didn't occur to her to take a swimsuit to the pool. If she brought it, she might not remember to wear it. Conflicts with the pool staff escalated because of Mom's behavior, and she was banned from the water aerobics class unless someone was in the pool beside her.

The idea of moving Mom from the facility near the shopping mall had failed; she still continued to wander off on her own. We discussed safety issues with her, and she agreed to call us when she wanted to go out. Then she did exactly what she was used to doing. It seems foolish that we tried reasoning with her time and time again. We expected rational responses she could no longer give us. Our frustration simmered under a veneer of patience. Clearly, she didn't have the judgment skills to keep herself safe.

Over the next several weeks, the facility phoned us almost daily to report Mom's departures from the building. Legally, they couldn't keep her from leaving, but they did try to help. When Mom walked toward an exit, they quickly phoned us, so we could talk her into staying inside. If she couldn't be persuaded to wait, staff tried redirecting her to other activities. Often we dashed to the facility, found her in the surrounding neighborhood, and brought her back.

One day Mom slipped out unnoticed, and we were called to come and look for her. After several hours, a stranger spotted her on a busy corner sidewalk, crying as she clung to a tree limb at the top of a retaining wall. He returned Mom to the facility, and *that* was it. Our family was exhausted. Staff conflicts with Mom had taken their toll on all of us, and we couldn't keep her from wandering off alone. She was moving to a locked memory care facility.

Later, we came to understand that our inexperience with dementia had led to poor choices about Mom's living situation. Mom was independent and opinionated, and we spent time trying to please her rather than making tough decisions. We were afraid of infringing on her rights and didn't grasp the idea that she was incapable of making her own decisions. Now we were at an impasse. Mom's safety needs were more important than her desire to be independent.

Making decisions for someone who raised you from infancy is difficult, and problems with role reversal took their emotional toll. We felt like children wanting to please a mother who was never satisfied. As it turned out, the right decision for Mom at the outset should have been a memory care facility that had more experience with dementia behavior and could offer more guidance.

Lessons About Choosing a Service Area in a Care Facility

What did these events teach us? We could have focused more on trying to help Mom adjust to memory care instead of making compromises in an assisted living setting that didn't really work. Mom was adamant about making independent choices, and we wanted to avoid a test of wills that would result in hard feelings. It had seemed easier to avoid confrontation and give Mom what she wanted. We simply didn't realize that it was time to put limits on her choices.

Our family's experience points out the pitfalls of getting an accurate match between a facility's services areas and a loved one's current needs. We didn't recognize the differences between assisted living and memory care, and we had failed to understand that Mom's dementia had progressed to the middle or moderate stage. Mom was *between* two levels of care and didn't seem to fit into either.

When a loved one is between two levels of care, one care industry professional advises families to choose the higher level of care—in this case, memory care—to help a loved one adjust before the next step in her decline. Waiting until the decline occurs will make the change more difficult. Another professional says that loved ones should be offered activities and tasks that add a sense of purpose to life, regardless of where they live. The psychological impact of moving away from home is difficult at any age, more so when decisions are made by others. Loved ones moving into a new environment should feel that family and staff are available for support.

We concluded that understanding dementia's progress and its final outcome are key factors in guiding decisions about care facility placement. Families with loved ones at home should consider this, too. While each person's dementia progresses differently over time, a stable living environment is the key to everyone's feeling of security.

When families must choose among multiple levels of care (independent living, assisted living, memory care, and skilled nursing), we suggest that they spend time previewing activities in each area. Facility staff may invite families to eat in the facility dining room, take field trips or engage in activities with other residents before signing a facility agreement. Don't assume that activities and services will be the same in all levels of care.

Memory Care: First Impressions

Previewing memory care facilities for the first time is often difficult for families. Many aren't familiar with dementia behaviors of others, so it's helpful for facility staff to prepare families for what they will see. Families should take note of this point: if a first visit is more about the family's reaction, it will be harder for them to evaluate what the facility has to offer.

To be honest, we were shocked the first time we visited a memory care facility. Few residents were talking, and the pace of activity was painstakingly slow. Profound silence filled the rooms and corridors of the building. People slept in loungers or quietly observed the day's activities from chairs scattered along hallways. Silence prevailed in the dining rooms, interrupted only by the clang of serving dishes or a radio playing soft music. Mom was loud and vocal—how would she fit in?

It would be Mom's third move to a new facility in three years. The facility's grounds were walled to the outside neighborhood, but residents could walk outside on garden pathways. When Mom discovered that she couldn't leave, her first reaction was angry and vocal. She regarded the facility as a prison and set forth with immediate plans to escape. She wrote angry letters to family and complained to staff. Her hostile response cast a pall over our family. There was nowhere else she could go; this was our last option. So Mom stayed, and the staff worked with her attitude.

Over the first few months at the new facility, we visited Mom regularly, and our appreciation and respect grew for the people who worked and lived there. Instead of feeling sad about our choice, we were heartened by the positive flow of energy in the daily routines. The facility seemed like a large, quiet family of caregivers and their charges, interacting in muted tones and gestures, each with responsibilities, all intertwined in personal relationships.

In the months to come, our contact with residents would dispel some of the earlier assumptions we'd made. Conversations were brief snippets, quickly trailing to a pause. Memories rose to the surface spontaneously, but lengthy stories were interrupted by gaps in memory and language skills. Some residents were articulate but could not initiate a conversation. Unsure of their reactions, we hesitated to make the first move.

As we came to understand the personalities of the men and women who lived in memory care, we learned that conversation patterns were mostly pleasant, but confusing. A woman, whose husband had died some years ago, approached one day for help with the telephone. "It's one long and two shorts," she said, referring to the old party-line phone system from the fifties. Entering into the moment, we escorted her to the front desk and asked the receptionist to put the call through. "I'll try the computer," she said. Then without missing a beat, "Sorry, but the line is busy." The woman, seemingly satisfied, moved down the hallway.

A former church pianist occasionally emerged from a cocoon of silence to play piano in the main dining room. All from memory, her music was beautiful. When she wasn't playing, her toneless whistle was muffled with soda crackers meted out by staff.

In the months to come, we learned that intact memories and abilities from the past coexist with confusion in the present. After lunch one day, a former nuclear physicist scratched out a solution to a complex math problem on a placemat. Sadly, in the same moment, she couldn't remember that she had just finished her lunch.

Several people in memory care thought the dining room was a restaurant and insisted on paying for meals. Staff was "in the moment" and no one argued with this. "The bill is taken care of," they responded. "No need to worry." Reminders about what is real and in the present can be reinforced with the aid of written prompts. A sign was taped to the seat of one dining-room walker:

- My meal is paid for

- My room is 121

- My daughter comes on Thursday

Dementia blurs time and space and dissolves social boundaries and controls. This unstructured attitude toward private space was illustrated by the facility's contingent of "shoppers"—residents who patrolled private rooms and common areas, lifting other people's belongings from closets and shelves. They tested doorknobs along hallways and entered unlocked rooms. Shoppers took other people's clothing, pictures, books, and other personal possessions. They walked the facility's hallways clutching stuffed toys or books. Mom's glasses, clothes, and other personal items were shopped with great regularity.

We responded with an aggressive labeling program, sewing her name into clothing, labeling artwork, and writing her name in books. Hearing aids were initialed and stored in the facility's safe at night. Glasses were initialed to make identification easier if they disappeared.

Many facilities are built with circular hallways to accommodate pacing. Hallways are punctuated with doors leading to the outside. Many residents paced hallways and garden pathways throughout the day. One walker dropped rose petals at the base of a white statue on a hallway table each time she passed. Tiny offerings were made all day long, petal by petal. Another frenetic resident wandered hallways, picking at furniture, curtains, and carpets. Sometimes she stopped at the front desk to do "paperwork" and consult with front-desk staff about her projects.

One resident was certain that he was a facility employee and often helped the caretaker with maintenance projects. Occasionally the staff wrote notes, giving him the day off so he could relax. In general, most residents sat quietly. An occasional misunderstanding might flare into an outburst, but it was quickly settled by staff. Caregivers did not argue with residents; they entered into the reality of the moment and resolved difficulties.

Families should be aware of the importance of entering the reality of the moment. Correcting a person with dementia or trying to ground her in the present may be frustrating and emotionally disrupting. Often, people with dementia don't differentiate between past and present. People who have died may be just as real and available as people who are in daily contact with a dementia patient. Telling a person with dementia that someone is dead may trigger mourning anew, as if the death had just happened.

The social calendar in memory care offered activities throughout the day. Game sessions and trivia were geared to slow memory loss. Group exercise sessions accommodated declining physical abilities. Monthly birthday parties and holiday events brought cake, ice cream, and live music. Sometimes communal cats or dogs wandered hallways in memory care, eating and sleeping in different apartments.

We came to understand the memory care culture and personality slowly, and we were surprised at what we learned from other residents and their families. Before, we simply had had no appreciation for what these elderly men and women were experiencing. Now we understood. For the first time, we met families going through the same transitions we were. We should have joined the facility's family support group earlier.

What Happens if You Live in a Different State?

Facility visits are new territory for most families. If someone lives in a different city or state, finding the right facility is even more challenging. A local Area Agencies on Aging[9] office offers a number of resources about facilities. Geriatric care specialists or hospital social workers can also help. Geriatric care specialists can provide support for families who live far away from a facility and are not able to manage daily care.[10] They can help with housing choices or organize in-home care services. They can engage loved ones in social activities and find local resources to address the family's legal concerns.

Two types of geriatric care services are available:

- *Private Services.* The National Association of Professional Geriatric Care Managers (NAGCM)[11] certifies people who can assess a senior's health and lifestyle, develop care plans, and help a family explore financing options for long-term care. These specialists work privately, and families who seek their advice pay for their services.

- *Free Referral Services.* National geriatric care franchises are available to help families with care facility placement. Commissions are paid by the facility the family selects, a fee often equivalent to the first month's rent.[12] Placement options may be limited to the facilities where the franchise has contracts. Selection may be more limited, and facilities under contract may not always be the best choice for meeting a family member's needs.

A search of state regulatory databases can also uncover information that will help families choose safe, responsible care settings.[13] Once selected, families should discuss communication arrangements with staff members. Facilities recommend using a single point of contact. The director of nursing has a finger on the pulse of activities and is usually a good starting point. Talks with the activities director determine whether a loved one is participating in activities. A set schedule for regular communication keeps the distance-care plan on the right track.

Lessons Learned

- Personal safety is the benchmark for deciding when families should take action to protect loved ones. Accidents can happen in a minute, and risks increase as dementia progresses.

- We concluded that the locked memory care facility was the best place for Mom but perhaps not entirely the right place from her standpoint. We realized it was more important to put her safety needs ahead of her wishes for personal independence. We feel that a facility's flexibility in accommodating personality differences plays a role in a successful match.

- Our search for facilities taught us the importance of finding the right place at the right time, depending on the stage of dementia. The right place may only be a temporary place. We think the emphasis should be on safety, as well as a care environment that allows residents to live independently, to the extent they are able.

- Don't be put off by initial impressions of memory care facilities. Before visiting, ask staff for a briefing on what to expect. Observe interactions between staff and residents to form an opinion about staff culture and the quality of care. Before someone moves into an apartment, make sure that it is outfitted with familiar pictures, photos, bedding, and mementos. Moving is difficult enough without the shock of a bare room in an unfamiliar environment.

- Don't feel bad if you can't resolve problems a loved one is facing. We learned these lessons the hard way. When we looked back, we realized that Mom's drive for independence was front and center in most of her actions. We could have done little to change that.

- Problem solving is really about adjusting your *own* attitude. Families cannot change dementia's course, they can only react to changing circumstances. Understanding this will alleviate feelings of helplessness and frustration. After placement, it's helpful to focus on the quality of visits and what the loved one gains from them—that someone cares and has taken the time to visit.

- A person with dementia has ups and downs. Things may plateau for a while, and everything may seem stable. This may be followed by a deep slide in cognition. A good memory care staff understands this and is trained to adjust to these changes.

- When someone with memory problems moves away from home, the move may be disorienting and result in a downward slide in cognition. Families should be prepared to expect changes. It helps to be observant and have flexibility in handling social situations in new ways.

- It's important for families to understand their own emotions about the changes taking place in a loved one's life. When a person has dementia, she *looks* like the same person, and it's easy to think that personality or behavior change hasn't taken place. Understanding the new person comes from being able to see things from her viewpoint.[14]

- Visit a facility multiple times before making a decision about placement. Talk to caregivers and see how they view their jobs. Talk to other families to find out whether the facility is a good match.

CHAPTER THREE

CAN WE AFFORD A CARE FACILITY?

*"I hope you'll have a chance to look at these revised cost
projections. I've prepared this report in advance of our
meeting so we can have a better idea of where we stand after
the 'point news' at the care conference."*

Family E-mail about personal care costs, December 1, 2009

No question about it, care facilities are expensive, and Mom was not going to move until we investigated the long-term costs. Costs, we discovered, are based on a number of factors: location, types of services provided, type of facility, and length of stay. The huge commitment of an annual contract left us wondering if the family could afford it.

Assisted living facilities emerged in 1981 as alternatives to nursing homes.[1] Assisted living facilities are less expensive, and they offer residents more independence and flexibility in getting the support they need. The estimated length of stay is one of the main determinants in whether families can afford a facility at all. Statistics differ, but the average stay hovers between two and a half and three years. We took a conservative approach and pulled together a five-year budget estimate. In 2011, the national average for a basic assisted living apartment was over $39,000 a year, a figure that will continue to rise in the years to come. Costs are even higher for those who need additional help with medication, bathing, dressing, or similar assistance.[2] Costs of at-home care, adult day care, or adult family homes are less expensive.

Paying for Long-Term Care

How does a family pay for these high facility care costs? Careful financial planning is one of the keys to ensuring that families maximize care dollars and get the best value for their loved ones. For us, this meant pulling together a budget to get a picture of Mom's income, expenses, savings, and assets. We also looked at a number of outside funding sources that might be available to help cover facility costs.

Long-Term Care Insurance

This insurance was introduced thirty years ago to supplement limited Medicare coverage for nursing home care. Policies pay for nursing home and health-care services, assisted living facility costs, respite and hospice care, adult day care, medical equipment, home modifications, and care-advisory services. Families planning to purchase long-term care policies should do their homework.[3] Most experts recommend buying policies at an early age because premiums increase dramatically with age. A good long-term care policy will have inflation protection to maintain its value. Two caveats: a waiting period or other restrictions may delay reimbursement requests, and the benefits may not be high enough to cover all costs.

Be sure to investigate the state's Long-Term Care Insurance Partnership Program,[4] a program available in all fifty states. The partnership program assures that long-term care policies meet minimum standards for policy benefits. A partnership policy also guarantees Medicaid asset protection.[5]

Reverse Mortgages

For family members (sixty-two or older) with home mortgages, this option may offer a steady income flow to cover long-term care costs. A reverse mortgage might be used to pay for care expenses, whether a couple moves to a care facility together or one person moves while the other person remains in the home. So that homeowners understand the risks and benefits of reverse mortgages, experts suggest they seek advice beforehand.[6] These mortgages may not be the best fit for everyone's financial situation. Organizations like American Association of Retired Persons (AARP)[7] and the Office of Housing and Urban Development (HUD) offer cautionary information on reverse mortgages.

Veterans Benefits

For those eligible, VA benefits may be used in conjunction with other existing insurance benefits. Eligibility is prioritized by financial need. Services are limited to certain care facilities and may require copays. Veterans may be placed in service priority groups,[8] but regardless of the group, people who are enrolled in the Veterans Administration health care system have coverage under the Uniform Benefits Package. A list of specific services is available.[9]

Aid and Attendance Pension Benefit

This Veterans Administration benefit is based on wartime service and a person's health, income, and medical expenses. People eligible for this benefit may receive long-term care assistance at home, in assisted living facilities, or in nursing homes. Funds may be available to offset care costs in a facility where a person is paying privately.[10]

Life Settlement

Some life insurance policies have provisions that allow cash-outs of fixed amounts. Before making a decision, be sure to seek expert advice in interpreting policy provisions to ensure the family has a complete understanding of eligibility and terms.

PACE Program[11]

Programs of All-Inclusive Care for the Elderly (PACE) is available in thirty states. PACE's goal is to reduce government costs by offering medical services to people who are able to remain at home instead of moving into care facilities. PACE is a comprehensive medical program that is available to both Medicare and Medicaid participants who live in specific geographic areas of a state. Medicare participants who don't qualify for Medicaid pay a private monthly premium to cover the long-term care portion of the PACE benefit. They pay a premium for Medicare Part D drugs as well. PACE programs may also offer free transportation to a centralized location for medically necessary services.

Income Tax Deductions

Internal Revenue Service bulletin 502 discusses specific rules for deducting medical expenses on annual tax returns. If a family member is *required* to live in an assisted living or memory care facility as a result of her medical condition (Alzheimer's, other dementias, or disabilities), the cost of room and board may be allowed in the medical-expenses deduction of the tax return. Annual certification of the person's health condition by a licensed health practitioner is required. Partial costs of some insurance premiums, medications, and qualified assistance portions of assisted living fees may also be tax deductible.[12]

Medicare and Medicaid

Long-term care benefits offered by these two programs can often be confusing. Eligibility depends on specific medical conditions or income levels, and program rules are continuously under revision. Medicare is administered federally, but Medicaid is partnered with state programs, and each state may have different Medicaid eligibility rules and offer different services. People age sixty-five and older, or disabled people under sixty-five, are required to join Medicare to receive medical coverage for doctor's visits, medications, hospitalization, and other benefits.

Medicare benefits for long-term care are highly restricted. Medicare will only pay medical expenses for a limited time in a skilled nursing facility or for skilled services at home. Costs of custodial care, or unskilled assistance with things like bathing, dressing, and eating, are not covered by Medicare. Current information about eligibility for long-term care benefits is available directly from Medicare.[13] Medicare Advantage Plans may offer additional benefits. Some Medicare benefits are available for medical costs incurred at home.[14]

Medicaid is a distinctly separate federal program from Medicare. The Medicaid program partners with states to provide medical assistance for people with low incomes and limited assets. Individual states decide which services to provide, what income levels are needed to qualify, and what type of personal assets will be included in determining eligibility. The income requirements for Medicaid eligibility fluctuate as new legislation is passed. Medicaid will pay for skilled and custodial care for qualified participants, although in most cases, payment is limited to nursing homes.[15] Medicaid may also pay for long-term care services in the home or community.[16]

Can residents of assisted living and memory care facilities qualify for Medicaid? According to the Medicaid and CHIP (Children's Health Insurance Program), "Forty-four states provide some level of Medicaid assistance to assisted living residents, usually through waiver programs."[17] Some states require care facilities to accept Medicaid allotments as full payment for room and board. Other facilities may refuse to accept Medicaid funding, limit the number of residents paying with Medicaid, or require that a person pay privately for a fixed period of time before accepting Medicaid payments. Find out about current state-by-state Medicaid program requirements on the Medicaid website.[18]

A wide body of literature addresses the practice of transferring financial assets to others in order to meet Medicaid's low-income requirements. Families should seek professional advice about the program's strict transfer guidelines, and have a clear understanding of the rules. Medicaid may challenge asset transfers, and it can place repayment liens on assets of an estate for those who receive Medicaid funds. Rules are complex and continuously changing.

Some families who can afford to pay privately make asset transfers to qualify a loved one for Medicaid, but the moral aspect of this practice is rarely addressed. We believe this practice is a matter of conscience. Medicaid's mission is to supplement medical costs of people who have genuine financial need.

Finances: Do You Really Know What's Happening?

Finances are a sensitive topic, and Mom was sometimes reluctant to share her personal information. We tried to be diplomatic, but we were sure she thought we were questioning her ability to manage finances. Unhappily, losing control of the purse strings is often the first step of losing independence.

Our own story may resonate with others who are concerned about a loved one's ability to manage. We thought our mother's finances were organized. She was a good money manager, she was frugal, and she didn't make unnecessary purchases. She was always careful in her business dealings and suspicious of anyone who might take advantage of her. She stood up for her rights and almost always got the results she wanted.

As Mom's dementia worsened, we saw a different sort of money manager. Her checkbook was in disarray, and paperwork was scattered in drawers and cupboards throughout the house. Piecing together her financial affairs wasn't an easy task. She was vulnerable now, and we viewed her unprotected lifestyle with increasing concern. She was living alone, and the media was filled with stories about scams against the elderly. Like many elderly people, Mom was easily influenced by suggestion. Paired with poor judgment, this was a deadly combination.

Our awakening about financial matters put the idea of care facilities in a whole new light. We now understood the security advantages assisted living provided. An apartment in a building with security precautions provides a barrier to outside predators. Seniors are much, much safer in a building that locks the front doors at night and limits access to strangers.

Comparing Costs: Living at Home or in a Care Facility

Like many people in their fifties and sixties, we didn't think to factor the cost of care facilities into retirement planning. Financial-planning articles seem focused on savings advice and supporting at-home lifestyles funded by annual withdrawals after retirement. People work hard to pay off mortgages so they can live rent-free in retirement. Our own notion was vaguely similar. We expected medical expenses to increase as we aged, but the sudden cost spike of Mom's unplanned move to a care facility was a wakeup call to look at our own finances.

Mom's mortgage had been paid off years before, and other monthly expenses were low. She was eligible for a senior property-tax deduction from the county, and if her income had been lower, reduced utility rates would have been available. Even though expenses would be less complicated with a single care facility payment, Mom's retirement budget was about to undergo a drastic change.

Gathering cost information about assisted living facilities would help us decide whether she could afford to make the move. Apartment prices varied depending on size and layout. Monthly rental fees included three daily meals, weekly cleaning services, bus transportation to local stores, and a variety of social activities. In Mom's facility, a married couple moving into an assisted living apartment paid a markup over the base price rather than a full fee for the second person. Couples considering a move should compare this cost to the cost of maintaining a home for one person and paying for a facility apartment for another.

We discovered that expenses would be simplified when Mom moved to a care facility. Instead of paying multiple bills for homeowner's insurance, taxes, home maintenance, groceries, and utilities, residents simply pay a monthly fee that wraps all these costs into one payment. Facilities may bill residents separately for cable television or telephone services, but often these services are included in the monthly fee. Mom's discretionary spending was sure to go down.

We found that facilities were forthcoming about annual price increases, and we used this information to improve the accuracy of a five-year budget. One facility had ten years of data on price increases, and another had three years. When we averaged them, we found a predictable increase of 4 percent per year.[19] Reassurance that cost increases were stable was one of three key elements in determining whether Mom could afford to make the move:

- the annual cost increases for rent and additional assistance

- how long she would live in a facility

- the impact on interest earnings as savings declined

Facility Fee Structures

In addition to apartment rental costs, facilities charge residents for additional services such as medication management, help with bathing, dressing, and eating, and other services tailored to someone's specific needs. These service fees are calculated in several different ways:[20]

- all-inclusive

- fee-for-service

- tiered

- a la carte

In a fee-for-service arrangement, all residents pay a similar monthly rate for an apartment, but additional services costs are billed to each person separately. A point system is often used by facilities to assign costs to these services, and families signing contracts with fee-for-service facilities should take note of the point system's intricacies. Appendix 2 describes the point systems used in facilities where our mother lived.

In a tiered-pricing arrangement, all residents may pay a similar monthly rate for an apartment, but services are apportioned into different cost levels, and residents are charged monthly in accordance with an assigned level. As needs increase, residents move to the next higher level, and the costs increase.

A la carte pricing refers to fees charged for one-time services. A la carte services might include charges for on-site use of cafés, hair salons, temporary medical services, or supplies provided by the facility.

Cost Categories in a Long-Term Care Budget

In addition to apartment rental and services, our five-year budget included other cost categories. Medical expenses were tricky, because future health issues were unknown. But health insurance covered most of Mom's medical expenses, and her monthly premiums were reasonable. After looking at Mom's medical expenses from previous years, we decided that they would not have a significant impact on her budget. We included a contingency fund for emergency-room visits in the budget. Other people might enter care facilities with medical conditions that affect budgets more dramatically. These conditions may translate into higher service fees, if physical difficulties require higher levels of assistance.

We included a modest allowance for movies, restaurant dining, gifts, and clothing in the budget. Personal care items like beauty products, Depends incontinence products, or latex gloves should also be included, because these are not provided by the facility. We kept our eye on personal items stored in Mom's apartment, because staff sometimes used them for other residents. Depends was in high demand, so we wrote Mom's name on each pair before restocking her closet.

Building a Five-Year Budget

Our first-year budget was designed around the expenses described in the previous section. We also included Mom's monthly income projections and came up with an estimate of first year costs. We used annual inflationary increases for large-ticket items, like apartment rental and services, to estimate costs for the next four years.

After reviewing the five-year budget, we concluded that the sale of Mom's house would easily cover expenses for several years. Renting the home wouldn't generate enough income to meet the high cash flow requirements needed to live in a facility. We sold the house, set up a contingency fund for emergencies, and laddered the rest of Mom's house sale proceeds into certificates of deposit. Staggering the ending dates of the certificates ensured that sufficient cash was available to cover monthly expenses.

At first glance, facility costs seemed overwhelming. It was easier for us to think of the cost *difference* between Mom's current living situation and the facility. We considered that taxes, home maintenance, and insurance expenses would be eliminated when Mom's home was sold. Grocery purchases would be reduced, because Mom's facility included a meal program in the monthly rental fee for her apartment. We also considered the amount of the cost difference that could be funded from sources of ongoing income, savings, and other assets. Suddenly, care facility costs seemed more approachable. A net worth statement helped us crystallize information into a pattern that was easy to understand.

What is net worth? It is a measure of a person's assets and liabilities at a fixed point in time. Examples of assets are: bank accounts, stocks, bonds, property, and personal items of value. Examples of liabilities are: home mortgages, credit card debt, or auto loan balances. A net worth statement is a useful starting point for figuring out how quickly funds will be spent down.

Table 1 is an example of a simple net worth statement.

TABLE 1

Net Worth

ASSETS

House	$250,000
Auto	6,000
Checking Account	3,500
Certificate of Deposit	<u>45,000</u>
Total Assets	$304,500

LIABILITIES

House Mortgage	60,000
Auto Loan Balance	1,500
Credit Card Balance	<u>3,500</u>
Total Liabilities	65,000
NET WORTH	**$239,500**

The importance of planning cash flow should not be overlooked. We estimated Mom's monthly cash needs by adding income sources such as social security checks and interest earnings on certificates of deposits (CDs). Then we subtracted recurring monthly expenses. By estimating monthly income and expenses, we could determine funding shortfalls at any point in time. These shortfalls would later be used to track reductions in net worth, a key calculation that determined how quickly Mom's funds would be spent. Our income and expense table might have looked something like Table 2 on the following page.

Shortfalls identified in table 2 can be used to demon-strate how quickly funds would be spent over a five-year period. An example may clarify this. Let's say that some-one enters an assisted living facility with $250,000 in assets. If their year one income is $26,000, and expenses are $58,000, the net loss (shortfall) for the first year in assisted living would be $32,000. Subtracting $32,000 from the initial $250,000 drops net worth to $218,000 at the beginning of year two. We expected that shortfalls would increase each year, but they were much less than we predicted. As a fiscal safety measure, we reviewed income and expenses quarterly to ensure that shortfalls stayed within our prediction.

TABLE 2

Income and Expenses

INCOME

Income	Jan	Feb	Mar	Apr	May	Jun	Jul	Aug	Sept	Oct	Nov	Dec	Total
Social Security	600	600	600	600	600	600	600	600	600	600	600	600	7,200
CD #1	0	431	0	0	433	0	0	435	0	0	440	0	1,739
CD #2	0	266	0	0	269	0	0	273	0	0	278	0	1,086
CD #3	355	0	0	368	0	0	375	0	0	381	0	0	1,479
Note	1,208	1,208	1,208	1,208	1,208	1,208	1,208	1,208	1,208	1,208	1,208	1,208	14,496
TOTAL	2,163	2,505	1,808	2,176	2,510	1,808	2,183	2,516	1,808	2,189	2,526	1,808	26,000

EXPENSES

Expenses	Jan	Feb	Mar	Apr	May	Jun	Jul	Aug	Sept	Oct	Nov	Dec	Total
Room	3,333	3,333	3,333	3,333	3,333	3,333	3,333	3,333	3,333	3,333	3,333	3,333	39,996
Points	420	420	420	420	420	420	420	420	420	420	420	420	5,040
Personal & Medical	1,081	1,081	1,081	1,081	1,081	1,081	1,081	1,081	1,081	1,081	1,081	1,081	12,972
TOTAL	4,834	4,834	4,834	4,834	4,834	4,834	4,834	4,834	4,834	4,834	4,834	4,834	58,008

SHORTFALL (monthly income minus monthly expenses)

	Jan	Feb	Mar	Apr	May	Jun	Jul	Aug	Sept	Oct	Nov	Dec	Total
TOTAL	2,671	2,329	3,026	2,658	2,324	3,026	2,651	2,318	3,026	2,645	2,308	3,026	32,008

The reduction in net worth resulting from annual shortfalls over five years might look something like this:

TABLE 3

Annual Reductions in Net Worth				
Year	**Income**	**Expenses**[21]	**Shortfall**	**Net Worth**
				$250,000
One	$26,000	$58,000	$32,000	$218,000
Two	$28,500	$60,300	$31,800	$186,200
Three	$21,000	$62,712	$41,712	$144,488
Four	$18,000	$65,220	$47,220	$97,268
Five	$16,000	$67,828	$51,828	$45,440

Amounts may vary slightly due to rounding errors.

In planning a long-term care budget, we considered the possible length of residence in a care facility—an average of about two and a half to three years. Just how much these years will cost will depend on a person's health and age. Costs will differ for each person, but a brief analysis like the one above brings the impact of a facility's charges into sharp focus. Regardless of how much money a family has, a budget will certainly help define the care facilities that are within reach financially.[22]

Not everyone will go to these lengths to monitor finances; some might think it's too complicated.

Budgeting for care facility costs is truly a personal decision for each family. Regardless of how a family views long-term care costs, it is helpful to have an organized system for tracking finances.

Every family has different financial goals. Our goal was to help Mom spend down her savings wisely, while making sure she had the best care possible. We weren't sure about future costs, so we tried to maximize interest earnings and monitor expenses carefully. One thing is certain for everyone: monthly payments to facilities are sizable, which makes cash flow *the* important issue. Regardless of how budgets are planned, families should consider strategies to ensure adequate availability of cash.

What if a Family Cannot Afford a Care Facility?

With smaller budgets, care options are more limited. Choices might include living with extended family, in-home care with outside help, adult day care, or adult family home care. Some memory care facilities accept adult day care residents. Community-based, adult day care organizations are another option. The first step in determining which option will fit into a family budget is to take a hard look at local costs.

The Metlife Mature Marketing Institute[23] offers a survey of state care costs that illustrates how costs stack up for different types of care. This survey includes nursing homes, assisted living facilities, home care, and adult day care services in each state. The relative costs presented in this report can help families zero in on affordable care arrangements, although calling or visiting local facilities is the most accurate way to determine costs.

If a private home is the care setting, and a family member with an outside job is the caregiver, there are hidden costs to consider. Quitting a job or cutting hours and benefits to care for a loved one is an income cost to the family. Suddenly, it seems reasonable to compare the amount of lost income to care facility costs for a clearer picture of the budget impact on the family.

Home health-care visits from approved agencies are another low-cost option for families. Finally, financial assistance programs or support programs are available for those who qualify,[24] and some state assistance programs may include reimbursements to family caregivers. In cash or in kind, these services can help offset the cost of in-home care.

Family Conflicts about Money and Caregiving Responsibilities

Over the five years our mother was in a care facility, our family learned to work as a team. Some things we learned were difficult at first, and other things came to us easily. Friends and members of our extended family with aging parents gave us helpful advice about caring for someone with dementia.

Many were concerned about the cost of long-term care and how to pay for it. Some families were worried about spending all of their parents' savings to pay facility costs, others were worried about their own ability to contribute financial support. Some were financially able to contribute more than others, and some were unwilling or unable to contribute at all.

Often, we heard stories about one sibling taking total responsibility for a loved one's care, while the other siblings contributed little. Some families were separated geographically, and those who lived closer to the dependent family member absorbed most of the responsibilities. In some cases, an aging parent moved in with one adult child, and the parent's funds were used to cover care costs. Tiptoeing around all of these issues fueled the fear that long-term care costs would spend down an estate, leaving remaining family members with small or no inheritances. Considering all of these issues, how should families handle their differences about care responsibilities?

For us, open communication about finances, a plan for social visits, and shared responsibility for Mom's specific care needs, smoothed out uncertainties. Responsibility for medical appointments, lunch dates, and outings were organized by weekly e-mails. One person took care of Mom's paperwork and financial matters, while another coordinated with doctors and kept track of medication issues. We teleconferenced frequently, sent e-mail updates about our visits with Mom, and shared care questions that arose with the facility's staff. These measures helped us keep close tabs on how she was doing.

Although two sisters had powers of attorney, in practice we chose to make group decisions about Mom's finances and medical care. We tried to focus on Mom's needs rather than push personal agendas. Mom's financial information was shared through quarterly reports, and her medical information detailed in weekly e-mails.

But if families cannot agree about medical or financial decisions, how should they handle their differences? If problems are intractable, the first step is to seek outside advice. Families might agree on a mediator or a counselor to help them work out a solution. If the disagreement persists, they might hire a mediator to review the problems and make a determination about how the family should proceed. As a last resort, attorneys or doctors may help families work out a legal or medical plan to manage care or finances.

These extremes might be avoided if families sit down in advance and agree on financial and medical-care responsibilities. Families might consider formalizing them in a written agreement, especially if they foresee issues that may cause discord in the future.

We found it useful to assess our roles as adults involved in a common endeavor: the welfare of a dependent family member. We tried not to let personal differences and childhood prejudices interfere with Mom's care. We also considered the future of our own relationships after Mom was gone. Did we really want to spend the next several decades regretting something that was said in a moment of anger?

Issues surrounding the care of an elderly family member are not difficult for many families. But for others, the Family Caregiver Alliance[25] is a useful resource for families who need help resolving conflicts. Contact them directly or visit their website for articles[26] and information about family conflicts that arise in caring for elders.

Lessons Learned

- Our biggest financial surprise was the high cost of facility apartments and services. Mom's personal care costs were based on a system of points that changed several times a year, making annual care costs harder to estimate.

- In determining whether a facility is affordable, it's helpful to ask people with local experience. Attend local Alzheimer's and dementia support group meetings to get advice before committing to a specific facility. Ask questions about what other families are paying for in-home or facility care.

- Our five-year budget was surprisingly accurate, and it gave us confidence that Mom's funds would be adequate to cover her care costs. We would recommend that every family prepare a budget that clearly identifies funding/income sources and estimated expenses.

- State regulatory offices and local Area Agencies on Aging[27] offices are excellent sources of information about care facilities. Choosing a facility that isn't a good match for a loved one will result in lost deposits, moving costs, and the general upset of making a change. It's better to do cost research in advance to make sure that the family can afford the facility that best meets a loved one's needs.

CHAPTER FOUR

CARE FACILITY AGREEMENTS

I t was the summer of 2006, and we had just completed our tour of local care facilities. Mom had finally agreed to move out of her home. The move was a major decision, a huge lifestyle change, and a big financial commitment. Was this really the right decision? We were all worried about the cost and how Mom would adapt to the change in lifestyle.

After finding the right facility, there was the prospect of signing a rental agreement. We had often signed agreements like this without giving them much thought. When we open bank accounts or sign up for home utilities, we assume that terms are nonnegotiable, and we accept them at face value. It seems that provisions are cast in stone, and salespeople are simply not authorized to change terms. These types of agreements make us wonder: Who is looking out for our interests? What about what *we* want?

On the surface, care-facility agreements appear to be similar to other agreements that cannot be negotiated. They are filled with standard language and contain a variety of forms based on state and federal legal requirements. But many facilities are flexible in helping families put together an affordable cost package. Sometimes they will waive fees or make special offers. Families can sit down in person and talk with staff about costs *before* making a commitment. Families have an opportunity to express their wishes, and they should approach sales staff with a strong grasp of family finances and with specifics about their loved one's needs.

Care facilities are willing to accommodate families. Most are private businesses, and they are competing with other facilities to offer cost and service packages that meet families' needs. Like many businesses, facility sales staff will present families with preprinted agreements. What can a family do if the costs or terms of services don't meet their needs, or if there's something about the agreement they don't like? Families should not be afraid to ask for concessions.

Flexibility in Care Facility Agreements

Cost is not the only criterion for selecting a care facility. If a facility has a quality reputation and meets a loved one's needs, a family's decision should not be based on cost alone. Many fine facilities are selected by families based solely on their reputation for fair dealing and compassionate treatment of residents.

Before signing an agreement, tour a number of facilities, gather cost information, and evaluate which services best suit a loved one's needs. The outcome will be a solid understanding of local pricing, amenities, and services. This can help families evaluate whether a facility meets their loved one's needs and the family's ability to pay. Resources describing national cost averages of facilities in different states are available,[1] [2] [3] but direct contact with local facilities will yield the most accurate cost information. Facilities often have flexibility in waiving fees and offering move-in incentives, so it pays to compare different facilities' costs and services before making a final decision. Some examples where cost flexibility may be an option are:

- NEGOTIATING APARTMENT OR ROOM PRICES— New facilities may offer special prices on apartments. More established facilities may offer a price break on the first month's rent, a trial period of stay, or other inducements.

- WAITING LISTS—Ask if there is a waiting list for the area within the facility where the family member will live (for example, assisted living or memory care). Absence of waiting lists may result in opportunities for flexible pricing, since facilities may be trying to fill units more quickly. A long waiting list may indicate less flexibility with price.

- ONE-TIME FEES—Identify one-time admission fees, advance payment requirements, or security deposits described in the agreement. If fees are not fully refundable when the agreement ends, it's fair to ask if a facility can waive one or more of them. Families should take note of cleaning fees, and refundable and nonrefundable deposits. When the agreement comes to a close, it pays to review the agreement and request any refunds that may be owed.

Talking About Terms with Facility Staff

It's important to keep in mind that an agreement must be a win-win situation for both the family and the care facility. Successful relationships are built on a clear understanding of terms and a trust that both the family and facility can successfully meet an agreement's obligations. Most descriptions of costs and services in facility agreements are fair, but sometimes they are not.

Often a written agreement is generally acceptable, but families might feel uncomfortable with some of the terms. For example, two provisions in an assisted living agreement that didn't resonate with us were a financial guarantee and an asset guarantee.

- FINANCIAL GUARANTEE. This provision required Mom's attorney-in-fact[4] to be personally responsible for monthly rental fees and other liabilities if Mom was unable to pay. What would happen if Mom was responsible for an accident involving another resident, or a fire in her apartment? If she had no renters' or liability insurance, how would she pay? If she didn't have enough money to cover damage costs, would *our family* be responsible if we made a personal guarantee? We thought so.

- ASSET GUARANTEE. This provision required a declaration that Mom have a minimum of $400,000 in assets. We simply didn't understand this requirement or agree with the amount. The facility's twelve-month agreement had a thirty-day advance termination notice that could easily be invoked if Mom's funds ran low. If our family were unable to pay, we would have been asked to leave. Given these circumstances, the $400,000 asset requirement did not seem reasonable. We understood the facility's concern with liability, but we didn't agree with these requirements, and they were removed from the agreement.

A family member with dementia may not be able to understand the terms of an agreement or participate in signing one. In this situation, the attorney-in- fact usually signs on her behalf. The attorney-in-fact is protected from personal liability, because she is acting as an agent under the written power of attorney (POA).

There's no obligation to sign an agreement on the spot. Care-facility agreements are complex writings, and they take a while to digest. We reviewed agreements at home before signing, a practice we recommend for the following reasons:

- It provides an opportunity to discuss the agreement with an elder-law attorney to ensure that a loved one's interests are protected.

- It gives a family time to evaluate the agreement and make sure all provisions, attachments, and exhibits are clearly understood.

- It offers a breathing space for families when tensions about the move may be running high.

Even if a family needs to act quickly, attention to detail and getting answers to questions now will prevent future misunderstandings about both the family's and the facility's obligations and responsibilities.

Care Plans

The care plan is an integral part of the assisted living or memory care agreement. It lays out the standards of care and services the facility will provide, and it defines how each resident's medical, social, and other needs will be met. Assisted living and memory care plans often consist of a preprinted checklist of services available to residents.[5] This checklist can be personalized with separate written instructions about specific needs (for example, help with cleaning hearing aids, help with exercise). Appendix 2 offers additional details about care plans and how their costs are formulated.

A facility's care plan may include a point system that defines how much time each task is expected to take. Each point has a monthly cost, so it is crucial to understand how the point system works. Points are assigned to cover costs of services—help with medications, bathing, dressing, eating, or toileting. The number of points in each care plan varies according to a person's need for these services. Some facilities assign points for each service separately, while others consolidate points into cost levels (for example one through ten points is the lowest cost level, eleven through twenty points is higher). Costs remain constant until the need for additional services bumps a resident into the next higher level of care. Some facilities do not use the point system at all—they include the costs of additional services in the basic room price.

As a loved one's needs for personal assistance increases, families and staff will review care plans together and agree on care requirements. Revisions go hand-in-hand with price changes, so they should be thought of as amendments to the main agreement. Each time a resident (or her attorney-in-fact) signs a revised care plan, she is agreeing to changes in services and the fees that go with them. Families should question increases in service fees if they don't understand or agree with them. Asking for specific examples of how care needs have changed helps evaluate whether cost increases are fair. But families should be realistic about this—we sometimes overestimate what a loved one can do independently. Nursing staff and caregivers interact with residents daily and may be more familiar with their changes in abilities.

Before signing a facility agreement, it's useful to determine whether all costs have been identified in writing. The family should review the agreement and all of its attachments carefully. Third-party vendors,[6] such as hair salons or gift shops, may rent space at the facility. The availability of their services may be mentioned in the agreement, but not their costs. Families can discuss prices and billing directly with each vendor. Sometimes vendors are paid for services directly by the family, but often charges are forwarded to the facility's accounting staff for billing.

Attachments and Exhibits to Care Facility Agreements

Large facility handbooks or state inspection reports may be referenced in care facility agreements as exhibits but will not be included in the paperwork a family takes home. They are available at facilities for families to review. Attachments or exhibits that might typically be included in a facility agreement include:

State Inspection Handbook. An agreement may refer to a facility's state inspection handbook, which records any notes made by state inspectors.

Resident Information Forms. The family describes their loved one's background, habits, hobbies, interests, and daily living patterns. Paperwork may include physician's orders, medical directives, and documents such as medical powers of attorney.

Resident Rights Forms. These forms include a description of a resident's rights such as the right to privacy, the right to be treated with dignity and respect, the right to control personal finances, freedom of religion, and other rights designed to protect residents of a facility.

Privacy Notice. A copy of the facility's privacy notice will always be part of the agreement. This is required under the federal government's 1996 Health Insurance Portability and Accountability Act (HIPAA). This attachment will be signed separately, to document that it was read and received.

Pharmacy Authorization. This form identifies a family member's pharmacy and the pharmacy's own privacy notice. It also acts as an authorization form to allow the facility to order medication for the family member.

Public Relations and Activity Authorizations. These forms are authorizations that permit a loved one to participate in field trips. A separate attachment might request permission to photograph a resident or allow her to be included in the facility's marketing projects.

Disclosure of Services. This form describes the scope of care or specific services that are offered by the facility. Each state's regulatory requirements govern what must be included in a facility's scope of services.[7] The disclosure of services helps define how completely the facility is able to address a family member's needs.

Where to Turn for Help

Most families experience few difficulties in working with care facilities. If differences do arise, the best strategy is to discuss them with staff and try to come to an understanding. But relationships are not always perfect, and if differences cannot be resolved, many resources are available to families for information and support.

State Long-Term Care Ombudsman Offices.[8] Each state has ombudsman offices responsible for assisting families with long-term care issues. Ombudsman volunteers are trained to help resolve residents' problems and complaints.

Adult Protective Services.[9] State and local programs are available to assist with issues related to the abuse of vulnerable elderly or disabled adults. Questionable living conditions or quality-of-care issues can be reported to these agencies.

Licensing Offices that Regulate Care Facilities.[10] These offices inspect local facilities and investigate consumer complaints. They provide information and assistance with specific issues.

Legal Support.[11] State-licensed elder-law attorneys represent residents and their families in resolving issues they are unable to work out on their own. Before hiring an attorney, ask about specific experience in handling the type of problem at hand.

Lessons Learned

- Many provisions in facility agreements are defined by state laws and cannot be changed. Other provisions, such as fees, financial requirements, or room rental costs are discretionary. Prepare a list of the family's personal and financial needs before discussing an agreement with facility staff and be ready to talk about the family's budget and a loved one's specific needs.

- Ask for an explanation of unclear terms in an agreement. The care industry often uses "terms of art," or definitions that have specialized meanings. A familiar word in everyday conversation may have a different meaning in a care-facility agreement.

- If the facility uses a point system to charge for care-plan services, ask about the frequency of care-plan reviews and cost increases. If they're combined into the basic apartment cost, make sure the written agreement addresses when cost increases may occur.

- Regulations governing care facilities are in a continuous state of flux. "The Assisted Living Regulatory Review 2012"[12] provides names of state agencies to ask about updates on regulations.

The foregoing discussion is a guideline about care facility agreements. It is not meant to be a substitute for personal legal advice. State laws vary, and each person's situation is unique. Consult an attorney for an explanation of how a facility agreement applies to the family's specific situation.

CHAPTER FIVE

ADVOCACY IN MEDICAL CARE

"I would be hesitant on how to medicate in this situation. The goal is not to medicate Mom so that she'll fit in. Some of the readings talk about people moving their elders from one institution to another, only to see behaviors repeat themselves. So I think we need to do some reading and get a handle on how to deal with Mom's situation in the context of what is commonly practiced in the industry..."

January 25, 2009 – family E-mail discussing proposed use of an anti-psychotic medication

Most people are accustomed to managing their own medications, and seniors are no exception. But if someone's judgment is impaired, what happens then? Some of our oldest citizens are making mistakes with powerful medications—mistakes that can have serious side effects. And they wouldn't dream of asking for help.

This attitude isn't surprising. Throughout our lives, we've taken over-the-counter drugs such as aspirin or anti-inflammatory medications without medical advice. Health conditions like diabetes and high blood pressure are managed with prescription drugs. We're accustomed to taking medications that we don't always understand; we just trust that they will work. Many of our older citizens come from an era where "doctor knows best," and they may not even question a doctor's advice.

In the United States, direct marketing of medications to consumers is heavy and relentless. Television infomercials suggest that you "ask your doctor if this medication is right for you." The family physician used to be the gatekeeper for pharmaceutical information. Now that has changed. Drug companies contact people directly with their messages. All this publicity legitimizes the everyday presence of drugs in our lives. How often have we felt comfortable with taking a medication because we've heard so much about it?

Sometimes a person with mild dementia may not think she needs help with medications, and initially we might agree. When a person sounds and acts perfectly reasonable, it's often difficult to believe a medication problem is hiding in the background. But it pays to pause and look carefully at how that person is handling medications. Remembering, forgetting, and reasoning abilities affect every medical decision a person makes. Can people *remember* to keep a doctor's appointment? Will they *forget* to pick up their medication? Or even worse, will they *forget* to take their medication and end up in an emergency room with a full-blown problem?

If someone is having difficulty with paperwork, household tasks, or medication, it's time to step in and lead her through the maze of today's healthcare system. Learn about her health history and prescriptions and determine how changes in memory and judgment affect her ability to take medications without help. Oversee medical activities and get involved in medical appointments, medical tests, and treatments. Most important, guard against the mistakes of others.

Unmasking Mom's Medication Problems

The opening chapter in our story about medication problems began with a visit to the doctor's office for a chest cold. Mom's doctor told her she had a bacterial infection and gave her a prescription for antibiotics. She drove home and stumbled into the house, leaving the antibiotics in the car. The following day we found her asleep on the sofa, breathing with difficulty, and rushed her to the emergency room. She was admitted to the hospital with pneumonia, and her condition was touch and go for a week. Finally she recovered, and the hospital released her.

The hospital stay unmasked problems with medications, and doctors adjusted the doses for several of Mom's prescriptions. We learned that she had congestive heart failure, a condition unfamiliar to us, and this revelation—along with Mom's failure to take the prescription for antibiotics—was a wake-up call. It was clear that she was unable to manage her own medical care, but we didn't recognize that this might be a warning sign for dementia.[1]

Many families aren't familiar with dementia's warning signs. A loved one may be in trouble, but changes in reasoning skills and judgment go undetected because behavior seems normal. Our conversations with Mom were light and easy—everyday topics about friends and family. We didn't consider asking her questions that would test her reasoning skills. We didn't know that she was forgetting to take powerful medications she no longer understood, and we hadn't considered the real impact of medication errors on an elderly person with impaired judgment.

Taking Responsibility for Someone's Health Care

After the hospital stay, we reorganized Mom's medication routine. We reviewed prescriptions, expiration dates and doses, and set up a management system. Mom routinely sorted prescriptions into a weekly pill dispenser, so we checked to see whether her doses were correct. It was sobering to think about the possible consequences of the many mistakes she was making in counting out powerful blood pressure and blood thinning medications.

We set up an appointment with Mom's doctor and familiarized ourselves with each medication. He explained the purposes, risks, and benefits of each, and he emphasized the importance of accurate doses. The doctor briefed us on high blood pressure and congestive heart failure, and he explained how particular medications reduce risks associated with these conditions. We learned how to watch for the side effects of these drugs. Older adults are often more sensitive to medications and drug interactions, he told us—something we hadn't known before.

We set up a system to monitor whether each medication was doing its job correctly. Periodic blood tests monitored levels of a blood thinner and determined whether adjustments were needed. Blood-pressure history ensured that medications were correct. Weight charts measured fluid retention and helped the doctor fine-tune diuretics if she had sudden weight changes.

Not everyone wants to know how and why particular drugs work, but monitoring how well they work is a necessary safeguard when caring for another person. Maintaining a list of medications and understanding side effects is critical to the safety of someone with dementia. Families should be aware of the consequences of misusing powerful prescription drugs, and they should know how to respond to accidental overdoses.

Families are often unfamiliar with medical conditions of the elderly, and they are surprised when they learn about the number of medications needed to keep medical problems at bay. Our family knew virtually nothing about blood thinners or the devastating bleeding problems that can result from a fall. Now we realized the benefit of understanding the side effects of medications, and we would begin to take even the smallest accidents or injuries seriously. Families don't need special medical training to monitor the risks and benefits of medications, just a sound understanding of the prescriptions their loved one is taking.

Monitoring a Care Facility's Medication System

When Mom first moved to assisted living, we were concerned about handing over responsibility for medications to the nursing staff. We had worked hard on perfecting her medication routine and wanted to ensure that it continued seamlessly. Each day, facilities handle medications for several hundred residents, using set management routines to ensure safe delivery, but to make sense of whether these routines are working, it's critical for families to be familiar with care industry standards. How can we know what a facility is *supposed* to be doing if we don't know the rules?

"Best practices" is a term used in many medical settings to describe guidelines or performance standards—in this case, standards for handling medication. Whether a loved one is living at home or in a facility, families can use medication standards to raise their awareness of safe medication practices. The Institute for Safe Medication Practices (ISMP),[2] for example, offers detailed guidelines for measuring how medications are handled in a care facility. A few examples of these guidelines include medication storage (security, temperature, labeling), cross-checking for errors, documenting and communicating medical information, and guidelines for staff competencies and training.

Whether in hospitals or care facilities, nurses are key players in ensuring that medications are delivered safely into the hands of seniors. Nurses follow a protocol called the "Five Rights"[3] to prevent medication errors. These are: "the right patient, right drug, right time, right dose, and right route." ISMP is careful to point out that the Five Rights are more than standards; they are actual goals for safe practice in dispensing medications.

A few examples might clarify how the five rights work in practice. In larger settings, like hospitals, patients wear identification bracelets. In other settings, photos may be used to ensure the *right patient* receives medications or treatment. The *right time* might include standards for a medication delivery schedule, and the *right dose*, the system for crosschecking doctor's orders, prescriptions, and number of pills dispensed. Families whose loved ones use time-sensitive medications should make sure the staff can accommodate schedules that may differ from regular medication delivery times.

When previewing care facilities, it is useful to be aware of medication practices that may affect a loved one's care. The director of nursing or other nursing staff, can explain the facility's safety checks and can offer examples of how they work in practice. In our experience, we think it's useful to ask specific questions when getting to know a facility's medication routine.

- Who monitors prescription refills, orders medications from the pharmacy, and determines that prescriptions match doctor's orders? How are charts documented to ensure that medications are dispensed properly?

- Who calculates doses and administers medications to residents: nurses, medication aides, or both? Must as needed (PRN) medications (aspirin or other low-dose pain medications) be approved by nurses before they are dispensed?

- What safeguards are in place to prevent transcription errors in residents' medical charts?

- Do medication aides' training and skill levels match their level of responsibility? Are all caregivers trained to recognize changes in behavior or demeanor that might indicate underlying medical problems?

- How often is the facility's medication system monitored by outside agencies for quality assurance?

- How frequently are residents' weight and blood pressure taken? Are both families and physicians notified about changes in medical conditions? Is information about prescription changes and new medications communicated to families by the facility or by the loved one's physician? Are charts accessible to family members who are responsible for medical powers of attorney?

A family meeting with the facility's medical staff to discuss these topics accomplishes many goals. It builds a bond of trust between the medical staff and the family and sets the tone for a good working relationship. A meeting gives the staff an opportunity to get accurate personal information about a prospective resident, and it helps familiarize families with the facility's medical practices.

Checkpoints for Monitoring Medications

Good medical care extends beyond the nursing staff in a care facility. For families safeguarding a loved one's welfare, it pays to keep tabs on the chain of people and companies that provide daily medical support. The working relationships among physicians, laboratories, pharmacies, and nursing staff can often be confusing, but the following checkpoints can be used to monitor what's happening in practice.

- OPEN COMMUNICATION WITH THE PHYSICIAN. The doctor is a key player in guiding a dementia patient's medical treatment. Families who communicate effectively with physicians will be well informed and prepared to ask pertinent questions about medications and treatments.

- REVIEWING THE MEDICAL CHART. The medical chart in a care facility is a health record that tracks a patient's blood pressure, weight, prescription management, illnesses, and treatment. Reviewing the medical chart periodically reassures the family that the facility's support system is working effectively. The medical power of attorney[4] is an important tool that gives families access to a loved one's medical records. The importance of securing a medical power of attorney while a family member is "of sound mind" and capable of signing it cannot be stressed enough. The medical power of attorney gives the family peace of mind, because decisions about medical treatment can be made for a dementia patient, who may not understand the treatments at all.

- LABORATORY TESTS. These tests monitor how well medications are working. If a loved one is having health problems, asking her doctor about test results will help clarify whether medication adjustments need to be made.

- WARNING LABELS. Facility nursing staff and families should review warning labels if new medications are prescribed, and nursing staff should make sure that instructions for dispensing medications are correctly charted.

If a facility's medication system is functioning correctly, families may not need to get involved at all. If problems are apparent, however, families should get involved and find out where the system is failing. If a loved one is living in an out-of-state facility, families may want to hire someone with medical knowledge to check up on the medication routine. Dementia patients don't have the luxury of even one mistake. They cannot object to medications they are given, and they have to trust that medications are being delivered correctly.

What Happens When the System Breaks Down

Care facilities don't intentionally hurt people. Their employees are human, and everyone makes mistakes. But medication errors *can* hurt people, so it's important for families to watch medication routines closely. Our mother, for example, had long-standing problems with one facility's medication system. After reviewing her lab tests, we discovered that her blood thinner had been administered incorrectly for months at a time. Her test results had been erratic, indicating problems with the dose.

A bit of detective work got to the heart of the problem: a breakdown in charting, and poor communication between nursing staff and medication aides. Fortunately, these problems were correctable, but often consequences can often be grave. Dosing errors with blood thinners can result in physical problems, including excessive bleeding (dose too high) to clotting (dose too low). Blood thinners are classic examples of drugs "with a narrow margin between therapeutic and toxic doses. They require regular blood monitoring and can interact with many other drugs and foods."[5]

Unless families have full confidence in a facility's medical care, they should be vigilant in monitoring its medication system. Medication aides should be up to the task in training and education. They are responsible for administering blood thinners, heart medications, and other highly potent drugs. State laws set training requirements and define limits of responsibility. In Mom's care setting, for example, medication aides were not allowed to calculate doses themselves, but they could assist nurses in setting up and dispensing medications.[6]

For the most part, facilities do a good job, and most families have positive experiences with medication management systems. A well-organized system and good communication among staff go a long way in reducing errors. Families considering a new care facility should check its state inspection records,[7] find out about past problems with handling medication, and learn what the care facility did to correct them.

Calming Drugs: Are They the Answer in a Care Facility?

Her anger continued, unabated, so we turned to a psychiatrist who gave Mom a brief cognitive test and wrote a prescription for an antipsychotic. Problems of a new sort arose—Mom was barely able to function. She sat in a chair all day, staring at the wall, unable to speak. After the dose was reduced things improved, but her speech and behavior were still not normal. Mom walked the halls of the facility telling everyone she was "retarded." Sadly, dementia had robbed her of the vocabulary she needed to express herself.

After several weeks, Mom's condition remained unchanged, and the antipsychotic medication was reduced even further. Then, a crisis. In the middle of the night, Mom swept through her room, knocking over lamps and scattering clothes and books. She put on several pairs of socks and pulled a blouse onto her legs. The next day, she was oblivious to the previous evening's events. A nurse suggested that this incident might be an adverse reaction to the antipsychotic. Mom's doctor discontinued the medication altogether. After that, Mom's anger seemed to have vanished. While this is only one example of a reaction to a medication, it illustrates the care that should be taken with older people's sensitivity to new medications.

Calming drugs do have a role in the treatment of dementia patients. Many patients cannot have a significant quality of life without them, particularly if mental illnesses exist alongside dementia. As with other types of medication, calming drugs should be judged by the risks and benefits they bring to the quality of a loved one's life.

Hearing, Vision, Dental Care, and Mobility

Communication is an essential tool in health-care matters; it affects almost every aspect of dementia care. But someone with dementia may not be able to communicate with others about illnesses, hearing problems, or problems with vision. It is up to families or caregivers to be aware of a loved one's needs, such as changing hearing aid batteries and making sure glasses are clean and fit correctly.

A lot has been written about the relationship between hearing loss and cognitive decline. This underscores the importance of regular hearing tests and hearing aid maintenance. People with diminished hearing find it difficult to answer questions and participate in conversations. Adding dementia to the equation makes hearing sounds and decoding complex sentences next to impossible. Hearing ability declines with age, and families should not be frustrated about a condition they cannot change. Audiologist visits should continue as long as the person with dementia can respond. Regular hearing aid cleaning and battery replacement are critical for dementia patients.

Alzheimer's and other dementia patients may experience a host of vision problems resulting from cognitive changes.[8] Understanding the impacts of peripheral vision loss, changes in depth perception, and inability to distinguish colors will help families modify daily activities to compensate for these losses. Eye exams should continue as long as the person with dementia can successfully participate. If a loved one has had cataract surgery, doctors can explain the surgery's long-term impact on vision. Ask eye care specialists for an explanation of how bifocals and trifocals may affect vision and balance.

Much has been written about good dental hygiene, and families should help dementia patients follow this advice. Many dementia patients need help with brushing and flossing teeth, and regular dental checkups should continue as long as the person is able.

As dementia progresses, walking without assistance becomes more difficult. Some medications may add to the risk, causing dizziness and affecting balance. As strength and mobility decline, furnishings in a living space can be modified. In Mom's apartment, we elevated her recliner with a wood platform to make standing up from a seated position easier. The bed was lowered to prevent falls, making it easier to get in and out. Throw rugs and obstacles were removed to prevent slipping and falling.

Lessons Learned

- It's important to learn about the future course of dementia and to use that knowledge to make informed care decisions in the present. Families should be able to recognize changes in a loved one's medical condition and know when to ask for help. Whether a dementia patient is living at home or in a facility, the ability to pinpoint the onset of medical problems is key to her welfare.

- Behavior issues should prompt questions about the possibility of underlying medical causes such as pain, undiagnosed illness, dehydration, poor nutrition, lack of sleep, or constipation. If a change in behavior is sudden or uncharacteristic, ask the physician about adverse reactions to medications or a test for a urinary tract infection (UTI). It's safer to eliminate these issues before determining that calming drugs are needed.

- When new drugs are prescribed, ask the physician about their purpose, risks, benefits, and side effects. Are low doses administered initially and tapered up as the physician determines how well the drug is tolerated? If several doctors are prescribing medications, who determines whether a patient with problems is having a drug-to-drug interaction? Finally, how long might someone need to take particular medications like antipsychotics before they are discontinued?

- Memory care and nursing facilities often have in-house physicians with strong experience in medication systems for dementia patients. If it's time to change to a geriatric physician, in-house physicians may be a good choice.

- No system for dispensing medication is perfect. Caregivers cannot provide continuous, individual attention to individual residents. Nurses and medication aides are busy, and errors are possible. Understanding safe guidelines for dispensing medication and intervening with questions can help safeguard a loved one's medication routine.

- Periodic review of the medical chart provides a check on how well the medication system is working. Keep communication with the doctor open and review all new procedures that are recommended. Check lab results and ask questions.

- We came to appreciate the hard work of care facility staff. They fill the roles of medical practitioners, social workers, psychologists, and group counselors.

- Reading and personal experience taught us a lot about health-care issues affecting the elderly. Our knowledge of frequently used medications, side effects, and medication safety issues helped us monitor our mother's health.

- Other families' personal experiences helped us keep our mother's condition in perspective. We learned that dementia is a disease, and it is terminal. When we understood the process of dementia and dying, we came to accept what was happening. Our quest to "make things better" was tempered with reality.

- We discovered what it was like to be deeply and personally involved in someone else's health care. The last two years of Mom's life were difficult for everyone, but we learned to be more understanding and accepting of changes in her condition.

• And, finally, we learned that loved ones with dementia are still people. They have histories, thoughts, and feelings. Many can express opinions, and all want to be treated with consideration and respect. For a person with dementia, life is a moment in time. What counts for that person is living that moment in a positive way.

The foregoing discussion is offered as a guideline. It is not meant to be used as personal medical advice. Every person's medical situation is unique. A family member's physician can explain specific medical conditions, drugs, and treatments appropriate for someone's circumstances.

CHAPTER SIX

HOSPICE AND PALLIATIVE CARE

"I really appreciate all you have done for me."

Mom's last full sentence, six weeks before she
died, June 2011

The final weeks of our mother's life were closing in, and our attention turned to the subject of dying. Death seemed to be shrouded in mystery, and no one was discussing the details. We hadn't thought to ask what would happen when someone approaches death, and now we were about to find out.

Professionals experienced in matters of death say that most families are not ready to *hear* about the changes that will occur until someone they love is close to dying. Because of this, some families don't look for support resources ahead of time, find out how they are paid for, or learn where to get information about them. How does a family request hospice services, and how does it find out whether a loved one is eligible? What can people do to comfort someone who is not in a formal program like hospice? If a loved one is living in a care facility, the answers to these questions may determine the quality of care she receives in the final months or weeks of life.

When our mother first moved to memory care, end-of-life issues seemed a long way off, and it didn't occur to us to ask the staff about specialized care or hospice. Later, only when her health began to decline, we investigated services to improve Mom's comfort and get answers about what was yet to come. Hospice, as it turned out, was a major resource, one that is available to all families grappling with end-of-life care issues.

What Is Hospice Care?

Hospice care focuses on a patient's *comfort* and *quality of life* rather than finding the cure for a disease. The hospice program, based on Medicare's qualification criteria, typically admits someone who has been diagnosed with less than six months to live. For dementia and Alzheimer's patients, admission criteria are based on a score of the Functional Assessment Staging of Alzheimer's Disease (FAST)[1] scale, which includes some of the following considerations:

- A person is dependent on help for most of the activities of daily living: walking, transferring from bed to chair, toileting, dressing, eating, and bathing.

- She has a limited vocabulary (use of six words or less).

- Aspiration pneumonia, urinary tract or other recurrent infections, or bed sores that do not heal are present.

- There have been multiple hospitalizations or 10 percent weight loss in the six-month period before admission.

The hospice team plays a number of different roles in supporting families and their loved ones. The team includes the patient's primary physician, the hospice physician, a social worker, the hospice nurse, home health aides, physical therapists, occupational therapists, and the facility's nursing and caregiver staff. Hospice staff are also available to help families with spiritual and bereavement counseling.

Hospice services are available in hospitals, at home, or in long-term care facilities. Hospice services are paid for by two federal programs: Medicare and Medicaid.[2] Regardless of the patient's health-care plan, the family can choose its own Medicare-certified hospice organization.

Qualifying for Hospice Care

As Mom's health rapidly declined, we received frequent phone calls from facility nurses about changes in her medical condition. The nurses also were in touch with Mom's doctor about her eating problems. Mom had always been able to eat solid food without difficulty, but now she was choking on food and liquids. After weeks of problems, the facility nurse requested a doctor's order for pureed food and thickened liquids.

Helping her with meals was frustrating. Mom ate a cup of pureed food at each meal. She could no longer swallow medications—they had to be crushed and stirred into her food—and she ate by teaspoons, often taking forty-five minutes at each meal. We wondered how much time busy caregivers had to help her, and we were worried that she wasn't getting enough food and water. Mom's eating problems prompted a flurry of worried e-mails among the sisters. At the time, we didn't know that a prolonged lack of interest in eating was an indicator that the end of her life was approaching.

The pureed food was a turning point for us, and reality set in. During one busy afternoon lunch, a dining-room aide plopped down three custard cups of pureed mystery food in front of Mom. We glanced sideways to see what other residents were eating, decoded the colors, and guessed that Mom was having a pureed tuna-fish sandwich and pasta salad for lunch. For us, the puree was an emotional turning point. We felt terrible helping Mom eat this food—a reminder of how she must have felt when she fed us as infants—but she didn't seem to care, and when she stopped eating solid food, the choking problems ended.

In March 2011, we were surprised by an e-mail from Mom's family physician, offering to refer Mom for hospice care. We'd watched her health decline over the last eighteen months, but the e-mail caught us off guard. We'd had no clue that Mom had less than six months to live. The sudden realization that she might be dying prompted us to look into hospice eligibility. We learned that Mom's facility had working arrangements with two or three different Medicare-certified hospice organizations in the community.[3] The director helped us select an organization that worked well with the staff in the memory care facility, a factor that would ensure smooth delivery of hospice services. The next step was to get Mom prequalified for the program. Medicare will not cover hospice costs unless a patient is prequalified by a Medicare-certified organization in advance. Medicare regulations require hospice organizations to conduct formal assessments before patients are admitted into the program, so we asked a hospice nurse to assess Mom's condition.

We were confident that she would meet the program's qualifications. In addition to problems with eating, Mom also required full care with bathing, dressing, walking, and going to the bathroom. She spoke only an occasional word every few days—one of the other FAST scale criteria for hospice admission—but surprisingly, even with all of these problems, Mom still did not qualify.

Qualifying for hospice care took on a new sense of urgency, because Mom's condition seemed to be deteriorating more each day. We were puzzled by the assessment, but hospice nurses quickly cleared up our confusion. Mom didn't meet all of the conditions on the FAST scale. Although Mom was fully dependent on others for everything and couldn't speak, she hadn't lost 10 percent of her body weight within the last six months or had a serious illness that required hospitalization. Our disappointment was palpable, but until she met these requirements, she would have to wait.

So we waited. Three depressing months went by. One day during lunch, a visiting hospice nurse noticed Mom's eating difficulties. The nurse, who was clearly sympathetic, reviewed Mom's chart and determined that her weight loss fell within hospice qualifications. Mom could now be admitted into the program after a medical referral from Mom's doctor, who was anxious to help.

His own mother had died of Alzheimer's three months earlier, and hospice had provided quality support for his entire family.

Once hospice received Mom's medical referral, the rest of the paperwork fell into place, and she was formally admitted into the program. We were relieved, because we would get more support and information about what Mom would experience in the days and weeks to come. At the time, we didn't know that Mom would die after only two weeks in the hospice program.[4]

Role of the Hospice Team

After Mom's admission to hospice, the floodgates opened, and we started receiving more advice and information. Hospice staff offered our family a unique perspective on the events that were to unfold in the coming weeks and gave us invaluable guidance for the emotional journey. For Mom, hospice meant the support of trained nurses, social workers, and caregivers who could help keep her comfortable. She would also be eligible for additional bathing services by a hospice aide.[5]

The advice we received from hospice helped lessen our guilt about Mom's inability to eat more than a few spoons of food. Mom's waning appetite was a sign that her body was shutting down, and we learned that we didn't have to force her to eat if she was refusing food. Families often feel guilty about this, and think that they are consciously allowing a loved one to starve. It was easier for Mom to drink health shakes than to eat, however, and the nurse said Mom could continue taking medication if she could still swallow. The nurse warned us that Mom wouldn't live much longer once she was unable to take medication.

When someone is in the final stages of dementia, she may experience swallowing problems, loss of appetite, and weight loss.[6] When someone's body is shutting down, she doesn't necessarily benefit from a normal diet of food or water. Ironically, residential facilities are required by law to *offer* food to their residents. But if someone is *forced* to eat, she can choke or inhale food particles, which can lead to aspiration pneumonia. At this point, successful diets may consist of favorite soft foods such as ice cream, shakes, or puddings. Thickened liquids can also be offered, but if a person refuses, thirst can be relieved by swabbing the mouth with moistened sponges.

Realizing Mom was in the final weeks of her life, our focus turned to gathering more information about dying. One of the best resources we found was a booklet titled *Gone from My Sight: The Dying Experience.*[7] It was filled with information about the different stages of dying, and suddenly everything became clear to us. Now we recognized the signs of approaching death that Mom had been experiencing over the last several weeks.

It was frightening to think the end was so close. Since Mom couldn't talk to us, we had no way of knowing if she was hungry, thirsty, or in pain. In the days to come, we would absorb a lifetime of information about pain control and other signs of approaching death. Not surprisingly, Mom's medical status was automatically listed as "do not resuscitate" (DNR) when she was admitted to hospice. No extraordinary measures would be taken to revive her.

In Mom's memory care facility, the hospice nurse served as the primary case manager. She was our advocate in working with facility staff and our educator in matters of how to care for Mom. The hospice nurse taught us to recognize signs of discomfort or pain in the final days and hours, a lesson that gave us the confidence to recognize whether Mom was having difficulties.

We should point out to readers that a hospice nurse is not continuously by the bedside of a dying patient. Our hospice nurse was responsible for many hospice patients in a large area of the county, and she spent the majority of her time on the road visiting homes and facilities. We think it is important that families understand this role, regardless of whether their family member is in a care facility or at home.

A hospice nurse relies on the family or the facility's nursing staff to watch over the patient when she's not on site. In our case, this led to a conflict with the facility's night nurse about pain medication. The confrontation erupted one evening during Mom's final hours, when the night nurse announced plans to give Mom a strong pain medication every two hours to "keep ahead of the pain." We were puzzled, because we didn't see the signs of pain the hospice nurse had described. Our phone call to the hospice nurse led to an apology by the night nurse, who came away with a better understanding of when to administer pain medication. We were able to work with him smoothly after that. The hospice nurse's intervention had ensured that hospice, our family, and the facility's nurse were all in agreement.

The hospice nurse was also responsible for ordering specialized equipment to improve Mom's comfort. An oxygen generator helped with breathing, and an adjustable hospital bed helped us change her position frequently. In addition, the hospice nurse coordinated family visits with a hospice social worker, an invaluable member of our hospice team. The social worker pulled us together as a family to discuss our bedside experiences and to find out how we were coping, which helped relieve our fears about Mom's imminent death.

Comfort Care for Dying Patients

Comfort care and palliative care are two terms often used in conjunction with end-of-life care. Palliative care, which focuses on the treatment of pain and symptoms for all diagnoses, is commonly called comfort care. Anne Koepsell, executive director of the Washington State Hospice and Palliative Care Organization, says this about palliative care: "It is a relatively new specialty and may not routinely be ordered by doctors for people with dementia, due to the patient's inability to communicate and the physician's lack of understanding of the nonverbal signs and symptoms of pain and other discomforts."[8]

Many patients can benefit from palliative care before they qualify for hospice. Palliative care transitions to hospice care when a person is thought to have a terminal diagnosis and is expected to live six months or less.

Palliative care programs can vary widely among facilities. Some facilities have formal training courses for nurses and caregivers, but most hospitals, and many skilled nursing facilities, employ social workers to help families navigate end-of-life care issues. Some facilities have no formal programs at all; they simply incorporate comfort-care measures into a dementia patient's routine care as needed.

To get an idea of how palliative care programs work, we visited a skilled nursing facility that is known for extensive staff training in pain medications and other types of end-of-life care. Hospice provides regular workshops for staff on end-of-life care to keep employees' skills up-to-date.

The facility's staff provides palliative care for residents directly, unless families specifically request hospice services. In addition to managing pain medication, the facility might offer services to improve the dying patient's comfort such as changes in room lighting, air overlays on beds to improve softness, soft blankets, and music.

This facility, like many others, provided food and beverages for families maintaining bedside vigils. Managers at this skilled nursing facility maintained that not every family of a dying patient needs or asks for hospice. Death is a very personal experience, and good palliative-care measures, regardless of the source, help ease the transition.

Can a family feel at home in a care facility when a loved one is dying? We think so. We had spent so much time in Mom's memory care facility the last two years of her life, it felt like a second home. We were on a first-name basis with the staff and other residents, and they seemed like part of our family.

In small ways, dementia patients participated in our family's experience, helping to ease our feelings about Mom's transition from life to death. As we maintained our vigil in the final days and hours, the door to Mom's room was open. Residents drifted in and out, oblivious to the drama we were experiencing. We didn't mind; rooms with no borders were part of normal life in Mom's memory care facility. The kitchen supplied warm brownies, and we shared them with everyone who visited.

The awareness of other dementia patients about what was happening in Mom's room, and the idea that we would interact with them under these circumstances, was truly remarkable. One patient, a former psychiatric nurse, sensed that our mother was dying and offered us counseling. We offered consolation to some residents, and others offered it to us. These examples illustrate that a family's personal experiences can be homelike, even in a facility.

Familiar sounds and smells can enhance a dying patient's perception of an environment that is similar to her home. The Illinois State Alzheimer's Association offers a brochure with suggestions for meaningful visits to loved ones in their final days. The brochure describes different ways of connecting with dementia patients who are unable to talk or care for themselves. Suggestions include using the five senses—taste, touch, sight, smell, and hearing—to comfort the dying patient.[9] Smells of home cooking such as freshly baked apple pie or cookies, tastes of a favorite food such as chocolate ice cream, playing favorite music or hymns, giving a massage, or brushing a dying person's hair are all examples of how a dying person can be comforted. These gestures can be comforting for dementia patients anytime, not just during their final days.

We followed the example of the hospice nurse and included Mom in our bedside conversation even though she couldn't respond. She was partially comatose during her last two days of life, but we'd like to think she heard our conversations about earlier and happier times.

The Importance of Educating Families about Dying

We think families of dementia patients should take the initiative to become familiar with information about dying well in advance of when it might happen.

Community hospice organizations, physicians, and long-term care facilities can help by making educational materials available to families, even when current regulations prevent a patient's admission to a hospice program. Although many families are not ready to think about the end of life, obtaining reading materials about what to expect should be at the top of every family's list.

Many resources are available from support groups, but a stronger hospice outreach to families, support groups, and facilities is needed to ramp up this effort. When someone is dying, the conversation should include elements that go beyond medical care, such as family counseling about what to expect when active dying begins. If families ask for educational materials about death and dying *before* services are needed, they can then recognize *when* to ask for services and avoid a scramble for information when they could be spending time with their loved ones. Hospice was an invaluable experience for our family, and we are in debt to hospice for smoothing our mother's transition into death.

"I think for some family members, the thought of hospice means that they are giving up. I would often share this phrase with the family members: 'You are not giving up, you are letting go. There is a big difference.'"

Pastor Bruce Dillon

Lessons Learned

- We learned the importance of prequalifying our mother for hospice services. Prequalification meant faster acceptance into the program because hospice already had her background information. This fact is important for families who are caring for loved ones at home and may be unaware of the benefits of prequalification. Also, Alzheimer's and dementia patients can move quickly from stable medical conditions into "active dying." Hospice prequalification ensures that services are in place, and hospice is ready to respond to the family's needs.

- When looking for a long-term care facility, ask facility staff about their comfort-care or palliative-care practices. Does the facility's staff understand the specialized elements of good geriatric care at the end of life, and does this care meet the family's expectations?

- After our experience with our mother's death, we realized why family support groups for dementia patients are important. Support groups are a pathway to information and advice about hospice and comfort care. We did not attend support-group meetings throughout our mother's illness, and we missed a chance to learn from other families.

- A wealth of information on hospice and comfort care is available on the Internet. If families don't have Internet access, local reference librarians can help locate reading material on these subjects. The resource guide at the end of this book lists organizations that will send free information upon request.

CHAPTER SEVEN

ADVANCE CARE DIRECTIVES

Advance directives are legal documents that define the type of care a person would like to receive at the end of life. It's surprising to learn that about 70 percent of us don't have advance directives at all,[1] an astonishing figure that should send a wakeup call about readiness to face end-of-life issues. It seems we are a nation unprepared to make last-minute health-care decisions at the most critical moment: when someone is dying.

Our research on advance care planning led to a confusing array of documents relating to end-of-life wishes. The living will, for example, is typically signed long before it's ever needed. Later, it's used by doctors to write medical orders that interpret someone's last wishes when they become critically ill. For the uninitiated, understanding legal documents like the living will can present real challenges, so it's important to be familiar with how they're used *before* an emergency arises.

Like many people, we didn't consider reviewing Mom's advance directives until she approached the final weeks of her life. We were prompted to revisit her living will, a two-page directive prepared by an attorney eleven years previously. This expression of her last medical wishes was confined to three procedures: choices about artificial nutrition, artificial hydration, and whether to use antibiotics. Mom had refused artificial nutrition and antibiotics, but had elected artificial hydration, and we were in a quandary. Hospice nurses had advised us that dying patients may not benefit from artificial hydration, because it could cause discomfort in the last moments before death.[2] We wondered whether Mom would have chosen this option if she'd understood its implications.

Families are often faced with medical, moral, and ethical dilemmas regarding the treatment choices selected by their loved ones. Most do not have the medical background to reason these things out on their own and must rely on the sound advice of physicians. An example of this quandary is whether to administer antibiotics when someone is dying. Some patients won't elect antibiotics as a treatment choice, because their quality of life would not improve, even if the antibiotics cured a life-threatening infection. On the other hand, antibiotics may improve comfort by reducing symptoms of infection in conditions such as pneumonia.

Shortcomings in the language of advance directives are often discovered during an emergency or near the end of life. The phrase "take no heroic measures" comes to mind for its vagueness, which leaves powerful decision making in the hands of others. "Take no heroic measures" might mean "don't begin life-saving treatment" to one person, or it might mean "stop a treatment that isn't working" to another. Advance directives, loaded with good intent, simply do not explain the reasons behind the choices people are required to make about their care.

Making medical decisions for those with advanced dementia is *doubly* confusing. The hard fact is that treatment goals and end-of-life wishes for people with dementia can change dramatically—long after they're able to make informed decisions for themselves. In Mom's final months of life, our experience with her advance directives revealed these limitations, and it changed our views about the type of directives we would want for ourselves. More important, we discovered that the conversation about these documents should include the family doctor as well as an attorney.

What are Advance Directives?

Traditional advance directives are legal documents that provide instructions to family members and healthcare providers about a person's wishes for medical treatment in the event of illness, injury, or incapacity. Their content and language vary from state to state,[3] but all are based on a premise that recognizes the fundamental right of adults to make their own healthcare decisions. This includes the right to withhold life-sustaining treatment if someone has a terminal illness or is permanently unconscious. The need for advance directives was raised in 1969 by attorney Luis Kutner, who expressed concern about the medical field's increasing ability to prolong the life of people in an incapacitated state. Kutner's proposal for advance directives took direct aim at the issue of artificial life support for people whose medical condition offered little or no hope for recovery.[4]

Advance directives may be combined into one document, but typically they are set out in two different types of documents:

LIVING WILL. This document allows someone to declare her wishes for end-of-life care *before* she has a health problem. The person makes choices about whether and how to prolong life if she is unconscious or her condition is terminal. The living will often contains specific directions to be followed by a proxy, or a decision maker, appointed by the person. The directions may include decisions about initiating emergency measures such as cardiopulmonary resuscitation (CPR) or artificial nutrition or hydration when a person's condition is terminal, or she is unconscious.

DURABLE POWER OF ATTORNEY FOR HEALTHCARE. This document officially appoints another person[5] to make decisions for someone else *after* she is incapacitated and cannot speak for herself. There are various names for the document and for the person with the legal power to make health-care decisions for another, in accordance with a living will. Sometimes a second person is appointed as a decision maker, in case the first person is unable to fulfill that role.

Unless people revoke their advance directives, the durable power of attorney for health care typically remains in effect until death. It can and should be modified periodically to reflect changes in a person's medical condition or treatment wishes. State laws generally require that both the living will and durable power of attorney for health care be made part of a person's medical records. Regardless of age, it's good practice to make sure that a primary doctor and family members have current copies of these documents. States may also maintain central registries where people can submit directives so they are readily available to all health-care providers.

Appointing a Health-Care Proxy

The bond of trust is the most important element when appointing a health-care proxy. Our youngest sister, a nurse at a nearby hospital, was our mother's proxy, the person legally tasked with making medical decisions on Mom's behalf. Her medical background was surely the reason behind the appointment, although a medical background isn't necessarily required for someone to be an agent. Whether family or friend, the agent should be prepared to honor a person's wishes, even if they don't believe in them personally. When a patient is in a moment of crisis, conflict in interpreting her wishes is the last thing she needs to worry about.

Even doctors aren't able to predict the complex mix of circumstances that may occur in the last moments of life. This underlines the importance of making sure a proxy is on the scene to interpret nuances and make treatment decisions that reflect a dying person's choices. Trust is the key to ensuring last wishes are honored.

When someone is first diagnosed with Alzheimer's disease or dementia, a proxy should discuss end-of-life wishes with that person while she is still able to make informed decisions. Dementias can last for several years, but someone's ability to understand medical choices will diminish over time. Conversations about advance directives may seem untimely or uncomfortable when someone is in the early stage of dementia, so engaging a third party, like a family physician or social worker, can help move the discussion forward.

Most people want to have a say in their future medical care, even at a time when they can't make decisions for themselves. The idea of having personal control, in fact, is a powerful incentive for persuading someone to sign advance directives before it is too late. Although advance directives may be revoked at any time by the person who signs them, someone with advanced dementia may not have the legal or mental capacity to do this.

What happens if someone doesn't have advance directives and is unable to make decisions for herself? In all but seven states,[6] laws identify surrogate decision makers who may act on someone's behalf without advance directives. Surrogate decision makers are listed in order of precedence: spouse, adult children, or others. Many states also set standards for surrogates making care decisions.

For families forced to make decisions in the absence of directives, having to guess about final wishes seems patently unfair. Many families lack experience in making moral, ethical, or medical-treatment decisions, and when faced with these difficult choices, they deserve to have a starting point. Whether secular or spiritual, making end-of-life choices for another person can have deep and meaningful consequences that last far beyond the moment of the choice.

Shortfalls of Advance Directives

It's easy enough to sign advance care directives in an attorney's office and drop them into a safe place until they're needed. After our experience with Mom's directives, however, we discovered that a more careful inspection of the language is warranted. Some states have advance directives that don't address emergency situations or lifesaving measures at all. Most don't explain the medical consequences of the decisions people are required to make. And as it turns out, the consequences of signing these directives are much bigger than the short paragraphs that fill their pages.

In fact, the medical consequences of the choices we make in an attorney's office aren't always clear, unless the attorney happens to be familiar with medical issues and can provide explanations. If people rely solely on the language in the forms, they risk making choices that result in unintended treatment outcomes. When we compared the language in Mom's living will to the medical advice we got from hospice workers when she was dying, the contradictions seemed obvious. We concluded that everyone should be talking to their doctors about end-of-life scenarios before they ever visit an attorney's office.

In writing advance directives, many attorneys rely on state laws that describe specific formats for advance directives—forms with general wording that outline a limited number of care options.[7] We don't often question our attorneys about these forms or consider how they will work in practice. If we took the time to reflect on end-of-life choices, we might have considered adding a description of our personal wishes to these prescribed forms.[8]

Five Wishes®: An Alternative to Traditional Advance Directives

Five Wishes[9] is an advance directive that was developed under the auspices of a national, non-profit organization: Aging with Dignity. It meets the legal requirements of forty-two states and the District of Columbia, but is used in all fifty states. *Five Wishes* offers an array of choices that extend well beyond those offered in traditional, state directives. It is a living will with an agent assignment, the two essential ingredients in traditional advance directives. But *Five Wishes* moves beyond the limited medical choices offered in traditional state directives and addresses quality of life, emotional, and spiritual matters, and an array of alternatives for end-of-life medical decisions. This expansive approach prompted one journalist to describe *Five Wishes* as the 'living will with a heart and a soul.'[10]

The *Five Wishes* advance directive was introduced in booklet form in 1998, and it has been available online since 2011. It was written in consultation with the American Bar Association's Commission on Law and Aging and other experts. Completed *Five Wishes* directives may be entered into state registries or in a national registry available to care providers.

Five Wishes may replace traditional advance directives in states where it is accepted as legally valid. The directive can be purchased for a nominal fee,[11] completed, and then signed and witnessed. According to Aging with Dignity, signing a *Five Wishes* advance directive revokes any current advance care directive a person may have. Differences in state requirements for *Five Wishes* are mentioned at the end of the form.[12]

Five Wishes can be completed by anyone age eighteen and older and signed at any time, regardless of medical condition. It is not a doctor's order, but if one is needed, and a patient is unable to request one, a health-care agent can use information in *Five Wishes* to complete other documents that can be signed by a physician.

Doctor's Orders: Out-of-Hospital Do-Not-Resuscitate (DNR) Orders

Five Wishes and traditional living wills provide instructions about a person's wishes *to a doctor and her family* if she's unable to make decisions for herself. A do-not-resuscitate order (DNR) is a signed doctor's order that translates a patient's wishes from the living will into a specific medical authorization. This authorization allows others to legally perform lifesaving treatments (usually CPR) in an emergency situation. DNR orders are typically written when people are critically ill, elderly, in declining health, or in emergency situations where life-sustaining treatments may come into play. The DNR order is used in many different care settings, even when the doctor who signed it is not present.

Availability of a DNR order is critical, because instructions in a living will may not be legally recognized by medical professionals responding to emergencies. Unless a valid copy of the DNR order is available, emergency medical personnel will begin resuscitation.[13] To confuse matters further, rules about advance directives may vary among emergency medical training programs in different states and local areas.[14]

The DNR order provides a clear legal pathway for emergency medical technicians (EMTs), hospitals, caregivers, and physicians to care for patients according to the patient's wishes. But not all states have enacted laws pertaining to out-of-hospital DNRs. Because of differences in state laws and local practices for handling emergencies, families of critically ill patients should investigate how medical emergencies are handled at home, in care facilities, or in hospitals before the moment of crisis is at hand.

An out-of-hospital DNR at the bedside does not mean "withhold all treatment" as many people believe. It instructs medical personnel to refrain from starting unwanted lifesaving measures such as cardiopulmonary resuscitation (CPR) or airway tube insertion. It does not stop them from taking lifesaving measures to prevent someone from choking or offering other treatments like antibiotics or pain medication.[15]

POLST: Physician Orders for Life Sustaining Treatment

The out-of-hospital DNR is a limited intervention form that addresses CPR and other life-saving measures.[16] So what other options are available for patients in emergency or end-of-life situations? In the 1990s, a group of Oregon doctors developed the POLST form for older patients or for anyone with serious or terminal illnesses.

The POLST form offers a broader range of treatment options and personal care choices than the out-of-hospital DNR. It allows people to elect trial treatments and to decide if they should be sent to a hospital for emergency treatment or because of an illness. Like the out-of-hospital DNR, the POLST is signed by a physician, making it a legally recognized doctor's order that EMTs and health-care workers must follow, even if the doctor is not present.

A POLST form is completed during an interview between a health-care professional and a patient or her health-care agent. Regardless of who conducts the POLST interview, the form is always signed by a physician. In some states, POLST forms are entered into a centralized electronic registry, ensuring easy access for technicians and health-care providers during an emergency. Research studies have shown that patients' end-of-life wishes are more likely to be followed if a POLST form is available.[17]

When to Take Action on Advance Care Directives

Advance directives can be signed at any age, but should be revisited as ideas about medical treatment and health issues change. When we're younger, our directives might focus on lifesaving interventions that support recovery. As we age, or if we have terminal illnesses, our view of lifesaving measures may include choices about whether to extend our lives using equipment like airway tubes or ventilators. Regardless of age, our ideas about emergency procedures should be relevant to our health, our spiritual beliefs, and the trust we place in the person making choices for us.

Decisions about advance directives are not just cloaked in private discussions between patients and doctors; they have the full force of the legal community behind them. A host of federal and state laws describe policies on advance directives that the health-care community is required to have in place.[18] Specific states, like California, have passed laws that require doctors to share information with patients about end-of-life options. These laws address hospice and palliative care, life-prolonging treatments, and choices about refusing food and water.[19] Federal laws require health-care providers to inform patients of their right to accept or refuse medical treatment and their right to have an advance care directive.[20]

In spite of all these legal requirements, the real impetus for making end of life choices must come from people themselves. Advance directives should be viewed as works in progress to be changed throughout the course of our lives. The American Bar Association, in fact, offers the "Five Ds" as a guideline for updating directives:

- Decade—at the beginning of each new decade of life

- Death—whenever the death of a loved one occurs

- Divorce—when a divorce or other major family change takes place

- Diagnosis—if a person is diagnosed with a serious health condition

- Decline—when an existing health condition declines, especially when it diminishes the ability to live independently[21]

With all this legal and medical support, it seems that we're not alone when it comes to making choices about end-of-life care. The structure is in place to dispense advice, but the choices are still individual and very personal. Hank Dunn, a chaplain experienced in end-of-life issues, touches on these personal choices. His publication, *Hard Choices for Loving People*,[22] is a comprehensive work about moral, legal, medical, and ethical implications of the end-of-life decisions we make. Dunn asks,

"Are decisions regarding life-prolonging procedures black and white? No! They are often shades of gray. As you gather more information, the answers will become clearer. Physicians, nurses, clergy, and social workers are just a few of the people who can help you sort out the decision. The medical staff caring for the patient will be as supportive as possible, no matter what the treatment decision."[23]

We agree with Dunn. Decisions are not black and white. A vast reservoir of information is available to help make personal choices and define the shades of gray. Advance care decisions, as it turns out, are more than just exercises in interpreting medical wishes. Moral, cultural, and ethical choices about extending life artificially come into play. Detailed discussions with doctors, family members, and health-care proxies can ensure that our end-of-life choices are carried out as we intended.

Lessons Learned

- Living wills and signed medical orders have different purposes. Living wills provide instructions to doctors and family members about a patient's wishes for life-saving treatment. Doctors transform these wishes into signed medical orders that give other medical personnel legal backing to withhold or withdraw treatments under specific medical conditions.

- The language in traditional living wills may be unclear or may not fully explain the medical outcomes of the choices people make. Living wills may limit choices about end-of-life emergency medical interventions. Living wills may not be honored in emergency situations outside of a hospital. If someone does not have a living will or durable power of attorney for health care, state laws provide for surrogates to make decisions on their behalf.

- *Five Wishes* is a comprehensive advance directive that offers a broad array of choices to families who are faced with making difficult choices about a loved one's end-of-life decisions. *Five Wishes* offers a guideline for discussing and recording both medical and personal wishes.

- Trust is a key element in selecting a health-care agent. When a person has dementia, an agent should help her complete advance directives before she loses the mental and legal capacity to discuss and sign them.

- Signed doctor's orders ensure that other medical personnel have legal authority to honor a person's last wishes for end-of-life medical treatment. Out-of-hospital DNRs are more limited in scope, while POLST forms are more comprehensive. Some state laws are changing to resolve issues about legal authority for withholding or withdrawing life-sustaining treatment. It pays to research local practices and determine how emergencies are handled in different settings like homes, care facilities, or hospital emergency rooms.

- Signed doctor's orders are powerful legal instruments that ensure our end-of-life wishes will be followed. This is one of the most important lessons that came out of our research. These orders must be readily available to health-care professionals regardless of the care setting. Participation in the hospice program provides additional backup support to ensure that final wishes are carried out.

- Advance directives should be reviewed and updated periodically. Updates should reflect a person's current wishes relative to age, health, medical condition, and ideas about lifesaving measures.

- Patients are not locked into advance directives and POLST forms even after they sign them. These documents can be revoked at any time, although someone with dementia may not have the capacity to do this.

- We regret that we didn't understand the purpose and the powers of advance directives earlier. We should have discussed them with our mother before her dementia worsened. We didn't realize that we would have to face end-of-life issues so quickly. Had we acted when Mom was still in the early stage of dementia, she could have explained her end-of-life choices in more detail.

- Our experience with Mom's advance directives inspired us to replace our own traditional directives with *Five Wishes*. We've advised our proxies to choose POLST forms rather than traditional DNR orders if we become critically ill. We learned that aggressive medical treatment may not necessarily be the best option for a person with advanced dementia. It is important for the family to be familiar with the natural course of dying and to understand the impact of medical interventions.

CHAPTER EIGHT

THE PATH FORWARD

What of *our* future? Will our care facility experiences mirror those we've talked about in this book? Chances are we'll be living in very different care settings than those of our parents or grandparents. A revolution is underway, and facilities are experimenting with new ways to meet our rising expectations for change—new living environments filled with purpose and activity. But the path forward is rocky in some places; as many facilities are still attached to traditions that emphasize medical and personal care needs over social and mental well-being.

Traditional facilities, with their clean institutional buildings and well-manicured grounds, are still safe choices for seniors, but are they really interesting places to live? Designed for work-force efficiency, these facilities are modeled around centralized areas for food preparation, medication setups, and group activities. The décor is usually based on predetermined design formulas, and buildings are furnished with period furniture and artwork. Personal adornments outside apartment doors are often limited to small mementos or brief biographies that offer glimpses into people's lives. The idea of a care facility conjures up an image of a sleepy place filled with walkers, wheelchairs, and people just "waiting to die." But some institutions are defined by corporate cultures that are very different from this. Not every facility will have us rushing for the exit.

Changing the Way We Look at Care Facilities

Innovative care models hold promise for changing managed-care experiences from ordinary to remarkable. Innovations aren't just limited to new facilities; traditional facilities have also stepped up efforts to personalize care for the elderly. They've become more than just medical service providers; they are redefining the industry with a focus on residents' social well-being. Although they're still saddled with older service-delivery models, traditional facilities have made strides in redefining the role of residents, integrating them into policy making and offering more opportunities for decision making. Similar to condominium associations, residents get involved in policy committees, field resident complaints, and have a say in the facilities' operations and activities.

The Pioneer Network,[1] a national umbrella organization composed of representatives from care facilities, government offices, and educational institutions, has been instrumental in contributing to this change. The movement's founders first transformed policies and practices in their own facilities and then spread the word about people-centered residences across the care industry. Many care facilities across the United States have retooled their cultures based on the Pioneer Network philosophy.

One facility, whose leadership helped inspire the Pioneer Network, offers an example of how this works. Its staff is supported by 275 volunteers who assist with social programs and run an on-premise thrift shop and sewing studio for residents. A day-care center is incorporated into the facility, offering opportunities for residents to mingle with children. Residents may mentor children in art, music, or cooking projects. An art studio offers residents a chance to exercise their own creative skills. Community kitchens offer space for residents and their families to prepare meals, a departure from entertaining families in centralized dining rooms.

The facility has a gym dedicated to transitional-care patients[2], and a library that offers Internet services and a magnifying reader for the sight impaired. In a salute to the times, wireless Internet is also available in all of the apartments. Self-service dining areas are open around the clock to supplement scheduled mealtimes. Residents are in the driver's seat in the day-to-day management of facility life. They participate in neighborhood councils and have a say in activities and company policies.

Dr. William Thomas, a pioneer in the field of progressive care models, has been instrumental in changing the way we look at elder care in North America. His philosophy, called the Eden Alternative, is a distinctive approach to elder care that has been adopted by many facilities across the country.[3] The Eden philosophy is based on a set of principles that guides facilities in changing ways they work with the elderly.

Eden Alternative facilities demonstrate how patient-centered practices bring independence and dignity to residents. One skilled nursing facility, for example, illustrates how the Eden concept works in practice. It's set up like a summer camp, with wooden arrows on signposts guiding visitors through the building. The building is split into "neighborhoods," with names like Ivy Lane, Forest Cove, Country Haven, and Short Stop. Short Stop is home to twenty or so transitional residents, while other neighborhoods may have thirty permanent residents each. Hallways and dining areas are alive with murals, and bulletin boards are filled with comingled photographs of staff and residents' families. The goal of the neighborhood concept is to promote unity between staff and residents, a goal reinforced with joint meetings and group decision making.

In keeping with Eden principles, the staff's focus is on the residents. Employees are permanently assigned to specific neighborhoods, a departure from traditional staff rotations to different areas of the facility. The advantages of this arrangement are clear: work-force stability, higher morale, and bonding between staff and residents. Staff members get to know more about residents in their care and can identify changes in behavior or medical conditions more quickly. Remarkably, the Eden philosophy has reduced employee turnover in an industry that historically finds workers on the way to somewhere else.

The staff stresses the importance of "giving back" the lifestyle and independence residents have lost.[4] The goal is to treat the whole person, the Director of nursing says, not just tend to medical and personal needs. Residents' lives are blended into the facility family, intertwining social history and experiences with staff. Residents are included in routine activities like baking, folding laundry, and watering plants. Gardening is available for those able to give armchair advice on fertilizers, plant maintenance, and watering.

In a departure from the thirty-day social calendars at many facilities, entertainment at this facility is not always on a fixed schedule. Entertainers might appear spontaneously in different areas of the building, strumming a guitar and singing. Carefully crafted efforts like this keep life fresh and interesting. Special programs like a staff member's on-site wedding ceremony and a separate prom night for residents illustrate this facility's commitment to integrating the lives of staff, residents, and the community.

The Green House Movement,[5] founded by the Eden Alternative's Dr. Thomas, is dedicated to providing skilled nursing care in smaller, homelike settings.[6] A typical Green House has seven to ten residents who live as a family, with a support team for medical needs. Certified nursing assistants (CNAs) act as the primary caregivers, with nurses and doctors playing supporting roles. Medical equipment has a low profile; lifts are integrated into the ceiling and emergency equipment is kept out of view. Green House homes aim for an environment that reduces stress. Private rooms are a cornerstone of the Green House concept, allowing residents to spend time by themselves. Common living areas with open kitchens allow space for social activities.

Elite Care,[7] a scattering of assisted living facilities in Washington and Oregon, offers Green House-style amenities to residents. While a typical Green House is home to residents who require skilled nursing, Elite Care provides multiple levels of care that allows residents to age in place. Elite Care is known for its pioneering technology in monitoring resident safety using global positioning system (GPS) and infrared (IR) technologies.

"It takes a village" to incorporate innovative changes into traditional facilities. Many facilities have found new ways to mainstream community organizations into the day-to-day lives of residents. Others have set up volunteer programs to work with residents on activities and projects. Still others have integrated outside businesses and organizations into daily activities. Over time, these groups become ingrained in the social fabric of facilities. Facilities are also retraining staff and reorganizing the way they work with residents, putting more emphasis on social and psychological well-being. Often, all it takes is a change in appearance, approach, and attitude to provide a refreshing new environment for senior care.

Whether it's the Green House Movement, the Pioneer Network, the Eden Alternative, or some other philosophy, the new attitude is about the resident. One expert observed that it's about normalizing, not organizing people by disease or function. Managed-care settings should mirror home environments, and the attitude should be about people rather than just medical conditions that require treatment.

Neighborhood Alternatives for the Future

Can people with dementia and Alzheimer's live alone in the community? According to one source,[8] there are some eight hundred thousand people in the early stages of Alzheimer's doing just that. They are supported by friends, neighbors, and families, who discreetly monitor their lives and help them stay on track. Living alone is not without risk; there is a fine balance between safety and an independent lifestyle. People with dementia who are living alone have a greater risk of injury and accidental death.

Families can take steps to increase in-home safety for people in the early stages of dementia: setting timers to turn off stoves or unplugging them altogether, providing microwaveable meals, curtailing driving, and encouraging walks with a companion.[9] Watchfulness is the key for those living alone, lest they fall victim to bad judgment from mail offers, phone solicitations, or door-to-door scams. When someone with dementia is living alone, families must be vigilant about personal safety and changing judgment.

Community support is essential for older people who continue to live in their own neighborhoods. To gather ideas about what people want, community activists in Seattle organized a series of neighborhood town meetings.[10] Most of the discussions emphasized transportation needs and the need for more in-neighborhood gathering places like coffee shops. Neighborhoods in Boston,[11] Santa Barbara, and Washington[12] have stepped beyond conversations and formed membership organizations to support seniors. Members pay an annual fee for help with transportation, home repairs, accounting and bookkeeping, cooking, and assistance with medication.

Dubbed the "Village Movement," communities across the United States are helping seniors age in place. Volunteers coordinate neighborhood social events, help seniors arrange support services, and provide assistance with everyday projects.[13] The nonprofit Village to Village Network was established in 2009, and provides training, education, and a clearinghouse for communities that need information to set up their own villages. The Village Movement complements government programs, like PACE,[14] that emphasize supporting elders in their own homes while providing outside social and medical support.

Dementiaville: The Answer to Future Care?

Some planners have tossed out traditional ideas about the physical appearance of facilities and have created designs to simulate towns from the past. Proponents of these designs think people with dementia and Alzheimer's disease will feel more at home in environments that mirror earlier lives. These old-time settings also stimulate long-term memory, a clear advantage in slowing the disease's progress.

To be fair, there is an ethical debate about whether it's right to alter present-day reality. Proponents think a familiar environment from the past minimizes frustration for dementia patients. Detractors promote the idea of reality checks for patients to keep them oriented in the present. Whatever the viewpoint, it is meaningful to dig beneath the appearance and look at how these facilities actually operate.

One example, Dementiaville, is a concept that originated in Holland for advanced dementia patients. Twenty years ago, a failing facility, Hogeway,[15] was rebuilt to experiment with the Dementiaville concept. Located in the outskirts of Amsterdam, Hogeway was transformed into a village with its own supermarket, pub, hair salon, and theater. Caregivers dress as shopkeepers, hairdressers, and cocktail waitresses, and play their roles accordingly.

Hogeway's 152 residents live in a social microcosm of the outside world. They are housed in separate living quarters that cater to particular socioeconomic backgrounds or cultures. Caregivers act out supporting roles differently for each social group. Residents generally believe that caregivers are neighbors or extended family members helping them out.

Hogeway's physical town is based on a bygone era of architecture, buildings, and layout. In a world where recent memory is a problem, the environment is designed to stimulate memories from the past. Avenues lined with trees lead to a fountain fronting a theater and other public buildings. Home interiors are designed to reflect social backgrounds, striking a familiar note for residents. One of Hogeway's main advantages is its protected environment that allows freedom of movement, reducing stress and promoting happier attitudes.

Aldersgate United Methodist Retirement Community in Charlotte, North Carolina, has undertaken a similar effort. Its Cuthbertson Village for memory care residents is designed around a midcentury town square with a soda shop, theater, and a variety of other stores that welcome residents. The village is composed of three neighborhoods, each with a secure courtyard and fifteen apartments with private baths. Like Green House homes, each neighborhood has common kitchens and other living spaces.[16]

The Alzheimer's Café

Eventually, elders with Alzheimer's or dementia will have to move to facilities that provide care for these conditions or in with families, who are not always equipped to care for them. Families who are caring for loved ones should avoid isolation and stay in contact with others who are struggling with their own care issues and questions about the disease. To facilitate this, a number of communities in the United States have established Alzheimer's cafés for patients and their families. The inspiration for these gathering places originated in the Netherlands in 1990.

Cafés are located in community centers, care facilities, or other venues that offer environments free of embarrassment and judgment. The cafés offer informal meeting places for families and professionals to exchange ideas. Their outreach programs draw in outsiders to discuss personal experiences, articles, and books about dementia and Alzheimer's.

Current and Emerging Technologies[17]

For those in the early stages of dementia or Alzheimer's, some families have turned to electronic solutions for silent supervision. These include web-cam monitors, motion sensors, global positioning system (GPS) equipment, radio frequency identification (RFID) bracelets, and button devices that can be used to make remote telephone calls in case of emergencies. One project[18] tests new in-home technologies—medication-tracking devices, bed mats, phone sensors, and door sensors—in real life environments to sort out how well they are working.

For those who remain in familiar home settings, these technologies and demonstration projects hold promise for extending time there. Fail-safe medication dispensers offer a solution to one of the biggest problems for seniors—taking medication at the wrong time or not at all. Other products monitor appliance use and provide automatic shutoffs, and still others provide remote backup in case of falls or injury.

Motion sensors coupled with remote monitoring systems are unique examples of how sophisticated technologies have become. Motion sensors—installed throughout the home—monitor sleep, movement, and eating patterns. The technology can also evaluate changes in cognitive function by tracking activity patterns. Some remote systems incorporate Bluetooth devices into their programming, devices that monitor blood pressure, weight, and glucose levels. These devices transmit information wirelessly from one device to another. In-home data receivers transmit data to health-care providers.

One system offers seniors a simple touch screen for social interaction. This same system also collects medical data, provides in-home monitoring, and uses a callback system for emergencies. Other systems are limited to data collection with sensors that notify watchers of changes in movement patterns that might indicate problems. At first blush, installation and monthly fees for these systems seem expensive, but each month in assisted living or memory care is costly, too. Whether these systems return value really depends on how long they are used and how efficient they are in sorting out false alarms with costly follow up.

For Alzheimer's and dementia patients, these systems offer only temporary measures for maintaining independence. And they may not always work in a patient's best interest, when direct human contact reaps more benefits. Eventually, someone with moderate to advanced Alzheimer's or dementia will need twenty-four-hour supervision because of personal care needs or safety issues.

This chapter illustrates only a few future possibilities for dementia and Alzheimer's care. We look to community groups, government organizations, and private foundations to change policies and laws that will propel these ideas into the future. There should be a sense of urgency about revolutionizing traditional care settings with innovative service models and training a work force sensitive to the needs of elders. The path forward will soon be well-worn with the footsteps of millions of new baby boomers looking for alternative solutions.

EPILOGUE

At a certain age, we start reading the obituaries in the newspaper. Maybe we want to see how old people were or how they died. Maybe we want to get a little glimpse of the kinds of lives they lived. Or maybe we are thinking about what our loved ones will say about us when we die. In July 2011, it was our turn to write an obituary—for our mother.

In earlier years, we thought—as many children do—that Mom would grow old gracefully in her own home. She would putter in her yard, visit grandchildren and great-grandchildren, drive to the mall, paint more pictures, and lunch with friends. Mom assumed the same for herself, but her life ended differently than any of us expected. She died as a result of advanced dementia.

As we compiled our collective memories for her memorial service, we came to appreciate that Mom had lived a rich, full life. Looking back at the bits and pieces we had gathered, we could see how she had influenced our own lives. Over time we had fulfilled the desire that most mothers have for their children: that we grow old together as friends with mutual love and respect for one another.

As we wrote Mom's obituary, we came to understand how much she had influenced our childhood and early adult years. Although she was no longer aware of it, this influence continued long after she was diagnosed with dementia. Indeed, the one thing she hoped for came true: our family bond grew stronger as we united in caring for her. Mom accomplished many things for herself, but the bond among her daughters was the biggest accomplishment of all.

APPENDIX 1

EXAMPLES OF COGNITIVE TESTS

Mini-Mental Status Exam (MMSE)

This exam is an indicator of cognitive impairment. It is a brief, structured thirty-item test that can take about ten minutes to administer. The types of questions on the MMSE can include:

- identifying the date,
- repeating the names of three objects,
- naming an object the test administrator points to,
- correctly following a three-step command.[1]

The MMSE is also used to follow the course of cognitive changes in an individual over a period of time and document a patient's response to treatment on a regular basis. MMSE test results also can help guide future treatment. Typically, a dementia patient's MMSE score declines by three to four points per year without treatment.[2]

St. Louis University Mental Status Exam (SLUMS)

SLUMS was designed as an alternative screening test to the widely used MMSE. Researchers Dr. Syed Tariq and John Morley, MD, created this test to screen patients with higher levels of education and detect early memory problems that the Mini-Mental Status Exam did not identify. It is widely recognized and used in diagnosing mild or minimal cognitive impairments or memory problems in the elderly.[3]

It is important to note that a person's MMSE score can be affected by his or her level of education. For highly educated people, the questions may be too easy, and for poorly educated people some may be too difficult. For example, a highly educated person with mild dementia may score in the normal range, whereas a poorly educated person with no problems in cognition may score in the dementia range.[4]

If your family member is tested for symptoms of dementia, ask the health-care provider if the SLUMS, as well as the Mini-Mental Status Exam will be given. It only takes about seven to ten extra minutes to give the SLUMS test, and it complements the MMSE by asking the individual to perform tasks such as simple math, naming animals, recalling facts, and drawing a clock and placing the hands on the clock. The basic difference in the tests is that SLUMS identifies early signs of dementia.[5]

Health-care providers routinely give the Mini-Mental Status Exam to patients who may be experiencing some memory problems or signs of dementia. Both the MMSE and the SLUMS are used as screening tools to determine if further testing should be pursued in diagnosing dementia.

APPENDIX 2

CARE-PLAN COSTS AND THE POINT SYSTEM IN ASSISTED LIVING AND MEMORY CARE FACILITIES

When someone first moves into a care facility, a written plan is prepared by the staff to define the type of help a person needs with the activities of daily living (ADLs). The care plan is based on needs identified in the resident's medical chart, an assessment by the nursing staff, and on information provided by the family. Many facilities use a point system to determine the amount of care and the cost of care each resident requires.

Care plans itemize costs in categories such as "help with medication," "assistance with eating," or "assistance with bathing." Each category is assigned a point value that represents the units of time[1] required for a caregiver to help a resident with a particular service. Each point has a dollar value, so a higher number of points results in a higher monthly cost for each service.

An example will clarify how the system works. Assume that a single point is valued at $60 per month. If a resident's total care plan has seven points, the monthly service cost is $420. If this cost remains the same for twelve months, the annual cost of services will be a little over $5,000. However, if points increase during the year as a result of changes to the care plan, costs will go up accordingly. Each resident's health is different, so it's difficult to predict care costs over several years. To estimate future costs, ask care facility staff about the cost of "full care"[2] at the peak of the cost scale.

To keep things simple, some facilities group care plan services into levels. For example, residents with care plans valued at one through ten points are billed a single fixed cost, those with care plans valued at eleven through twenty points are billed a higher fixed cost, and so forth. This system of billing levels simplifies things by eliminating the need for frequent price changes as care needs fluctuate.

Some examples of care-plan cost categories are:

- dispensing oral medication or providing special help with medical equipment like oxygen tanks, nebulizers, or inhalers;

- help with medical treatments like administering drops, dressings, and ointments;

- help with bathing, dressing, toileting, and other personal services;

- providing for special dietary needs such as pureed food;

- allocating extra time for communicating with residents (due to hearing loss or inability to understand directions); and

- helping residents transfer to and from wheel-chairs, walkers, beds, or toilets.

A facility also provides other services that are not included in care plans. Things like meals and apartment cleaning are usually wrapped into the room rental price. What's included in the room rental price may vary though, so families should ask for specifics. Personal laundry, for example, may be excluded in assisted living, but included in memory care.

Monthly care-plan costs are often invoiced separately from room or apartment rental costs, making it easier to identify medical-care expenses. Families should be aware of Internal Revenue Service (IRS) publication 502, which describes which facility living expenses are eligible for tax deductions.

APPENDIX 3

TECHNOLOGIES—NOW AND THE FUTURE

In-Home Remote Monitoring Technologies

Center for Aging Services Technology (CAST). A program of the American Association of Homes and Services for the Aging, 2519 Connecticut Avenue NW, Washington, DC 20008-1520, Phone (202) 508-9416, www.agingtech. org (*Imagine—The Future of Aging: Vision Video Introductory Guide*). Video summarizes information about existing and emerging technologies for remote monitoring.

The eNeighbor Remote Monitoring System. 1191 Northland Dr., Mendota Heights, MN 55120, phone 800-576-1779, www.healthsense.com. The system monitors patterns of activity using remote monitoring sensors (not cameras), such as motion detectors, and reports unusual patterns of activities. The system is also capable of integrating with vital sign monitoring devices and has other capabilities to assist with medication.

GrandCare Systems. 327 N. Main St., Lower Riverside, West Bend, WI 53095, phone 262-338-6147, www.grandcare.com. This company provides interactive touch screen devices for elders living alone. The system has different modules, but includes an easy e-mail system, games, and video conferencing capability for caregivers and family. The system uses Bluetooth (wireless) technologies to monitor weight, blood pressure, and glucose, and to chart data for remote and in-home use. The system also includes modules for prescription dispensing, including pictures of pills and requirements for taking medications.

"Sensors Help Keep the Elderly Safe, and at Home." The *New York Times*, February 12, 2009, www.nytimes.com/2009. This comprehensive article describes the ins and outs of wireless sensors and motion detectors used with central monitoring systems. The article describes the benefits, the technology, emerging issues with reimbursement, and social shortcomings of the systems.

Sutter, John D. "Sensors monitor older people at home." CNN Labs, November 19, 2010, www.CNN.com/2010/TECH/innovation. This article is a story of a senior citizen in Columbia, South Carolina, who describes the ins and outs of the GrandCare System. This is another comprehensive article that discusses on the ground and emerging technology issues.

Tracking Technologies

RFID Tracking Systems. RFID bracelets are used by law enforcement programs to track wandering seniors. Using a base receiver and the person's last known location, officers can track a bracelet within a limited geographical area, including inside homes or shopping malls. Bracelets are waterproof and cannot be removed.

GPS Tracking Systems. These systems require the transmitter to be on the person's clothing, attached to a belt, or in a purse or bag. For Alzheimer's and other dementia patients, it will not work if the person leaves without the transmitter. GPS tracking does not penetrate buildings, but it has a broad geographic advantage over an RFID system. GPS transmitters can also be used with software packages that allow users to set perimeters around a home or facility and send notifications to family and caregivers if the perimeter is breached.

UnLoc Smart Phone Locator. This is an indoor location technology in development. It can be used on smart phones to navigate inside a building, similar to GPS outside a building. Nordstrom, Kerstin, "Indoor directions for phones go beyond GPS," The (Tacoma) *News Tribune,* July 15, 2012.

Emergency Pendants. Emergency pendants may be purchased from a variety of companies that provide equipment and services for the elderly. Worn as a necklace or bracelet, pendants summon help with the push of a button. Users may program family telephone numbers into the system's receiver. If the button is pushed, the systems rotates through a set list of telephone numbers until it reaches a live party. These pendants may be set up for use by families and neighbors. There are no monthly fees. Private companies also sell pendants and bracelets with monitoring services for a monthly fee. Both types are widely advertised on the Internet.

Home Safety

This Caring Home, www.thiscaringhome.com. This website offers tips and tools to enhance home safety for Alzheimer's and dementia patients. It offers readers an excellent summary of inexpensive, low-tech devices, such as stove turnoff timers, plug-in timers for appliances, and toaster oven keyboard locks. Clever tips for safety proofing homes and suggestions for keeping patients from wandering out of the home are available.

Assistive Products

Medication Monitoring. A variety of these products are available. They include locking pill boxes with reminder systems, some capable of being monitored remotely for compliance. For an example, visit Honeywell's HomMed Life Stream Solutions at www.hommed.com.

RFID Memory Mirror. Georgia Institute of Technology, and CareGiver's Assistant, Intel Research Seattle, www. wired.com/medtech/healthnews. These two institutions have developed RFID tags that identify medications and track when they are used. Movement is recorded by RFID readers and capable of remote access.

Oregon Health & Science University, www.orcatech.org. This website describes a variety of projects that evaluate elders for dementia. Information about products for in-home monitoring is also available. One program, the Living Lab, is managed in cooperation with seniors and facilities in the Portland, Oregon area. The Living Lab "explores technologies to support independent living," behavior changes, and a variety of other topics.

Intel and General Electric Corporation partnership. This cooperative venture promises an exploration into a number of monitoring and device technologies to assist people at home. A launch video is available at www.intel. com, intelstudios.edgesuite.net.

Cognitive Fitness Technologies

PositScience, www.positscience.com. This website offers exercises in language, concentration, and executive function. Software can be installed on a PC.

Dakim Brain Fitness, www.dakim.com. This website offers cognitive assessment and fitness games for improving memory, language, computation, and critical thinking. Games have specific historical and generational references.

Education

*HomeInsteadSeniorCare,*www.helpforalzheimersfamilies. com. This website offers complimentary education about Alzheimer's and dementia.

The SCAN Foundation. This independent, charitable organization offers information about long-term care services and support available to keep seniors independent in their communities. Go to www.thescanfoundation.org and look at fact sheets under the publications tab.

RESOURCES

General Resources

US Department of Health and Human Services, Administration on Aging

The department has an elder-care locator by zip code, as well as links to local agencies, facilities, and resources. The website lists contact information and links to dozens of programs and studies relevant to care issues about older adults. US DHHS, Administration on Aging, 1 Massachusetts Avenue NW, Washington, DC 20001. Phone 800-677-1116 or visit website at www.aoa.gov. For elder care locator, go to www.eldercare.gov or call 800-677-1116.

National Association of Area Agencies on Aging (AAA)

Area Agencies on Aging (AAAs) were established under the Older Americans Act in 1973. This organization's goal is to help Americans over age sixty find home and community services to help them remain in their homes as long as possible. Title VI Native American aging programs for older American Indians, Alaska Natives, and Native Hawaiians are also available. AAA, 1730 Rhode Island Avenue NW, Suite 1200, Washington, DC 20036. Phone 202-872-0888. State and local contact lists are available online for a variety of programs and resources at www.n4a.org. Click on interactive map under "Answers on Aging" and find your local AAA or Title VI Native American aging program.

Family Caregiver Alliance

This organization provides information about caregiving issues for families. Its website has a state-by-state family navigator link to state agencies that provide support to caregivers. The website offers a comprehensive list of organizations that covers topics about aging and elder abuse and offers information about caregiver resources, resource locators, and disease-specific organizations. For those families with a loved one who is a California resident, this organization sponsors Link2Care, a family resource center on dementia caregiving with online forums, webinars on elder care, and information resources. Contact Link2care@caregiver.org or call the Family Caregiver Alliance main telephone number for more information. National Center on Caregiving, 785 Market Street, Suite 750, San Francisco, CA 94013. Phone 415-434-3388 or 800-445-8106 or go to www.caregiver.org and click on "fact sheets and publications."

Chapter One: Coming to Terms with Dementia

Alzheimer's Association

The Alzheimer's Association provides a comprehensive list of topics related to Alzheimer's disease on their website. Go to www.alz.org/physicians or call 800-272-3900 for more information.

Helpguide.org

This organization offers informative, easy to understand articles about symptoms of Alzheimer's disease, early warning signs, care planning, age-related memory loss, and a full spectrum of topics related to Alzheimer's disease. Go to www.helpguide.org and click on "After 50" then "Alzheimer's & Dementia" in the left sidebar.

Johns Hopkins Medicine

Free *Guide to Understanding Dementia* publication discusses dementia diagnoses and describes how to distinguish among normal 'senior moments,' mild cognitive impairment, and dementia. Also describes simple tests for cognitive impairment. To order, enter *Guide to Understanding Dementia* in a Google search window. Go to: JohnsHopkinsHealthAlerts.com for other reports and research on dementia and Alzheimer's disease.

Teepa Snow

Teepa Snow is a certified occupational therapist who trains and consults for healthcare professionals and families. Her website, Meet Teepa Snow, provides links to a variety of Internet resources and books on dementia. Go to teepasnow.com for general information. For video clips, type "Teepa Snow YouTube videos" into a Google search window. Ms. Snow's insight into the medical underpinnings of dementia and Alzheimer's disease and her work in interpreting the disease from the patient's viewpoint open new doors for families trying to understand dementia.

Understanding the Dementia Experience

This informative, twenty-eight-page publication describes the dementia experience in lay terms. It includes a discussion of short and long-term memory and a description of thinking, feelings, and reactions from an Alzheimer patient's viewpoint. The publication has excellent information on Alzheimer's care and on handling new and sometimes difficult situations. Jennifer Ghent-Fuller, BA, RN, MScN. To view a complimentary copy, go to Smashwords, https:// www.smashwords.com/books/view/210580#download or Barnes & Noble at http://www.barnesandnoble.com/w/ understanding-the-dementia-experience-jennifer-ghent-fuller/1113743329?ean=2940045020589.

Still Alice

This book describes the life of a Harvard professor after her diagnosis with early-onset Alzheimer's disease. Events in Alice's professional and family life offer readers a realistic look at the confusion experienced from the viewpoint of a person with Alzheimer's. Readers gain insight about Alzheimer's disease through descriptions of Alice's memory lapses and her efforts to cope with the changes taking place in her career and home life. Lisa Genova, PhD. *Still Alice* is available in bookstores and at www.Amazon.com.

Chapter Two: Care Facilities: Making the Right Move

Brightfocus Foundation

This organization is a resource for the latest information about Alzheimer's research and news. The website has a comprehensive listing of national resources available for just about every organization that can offer assistance related to Alzheimer's and dementia care. The website also has fact sheets, a booklist, and a tab for memory games. For information, go to www.brightfocus.org and click on "Find Useful Resources" and "Alzheimer's Disease Resources." Call 800-437-2423 or 301-948-3294 for information.

Dementia and Driving

Articles and publications about driving and dementia are available at seniordriving.aaa.com: "We Need to Talk: Family Conversations with Older Drivers," "At the Crossroads: A Guide to Alzheimer's Disease," and "AAA Drivers 55 Plus Handbook." AAA also offers AAA Roadwise Review—A Tool to Help Seniors Drive Safely Longer (computer based self-screening tool). Publications can be accessed by name in Google search windows. Phone 800-562-2582 for information.

National Association of Professional Geriatric Care Managers (NAPGCM)

Geriatric care managers provide assistance in evaluating an elder's care needs. They help families make choices about housing options, social activities, and safety needs. They also help with legal and financial activities, home-care management, and individual care plans. Geriatric care managers are an important local resource for families who live some distance from their loved ones. The NAPGCM website has links to the organization's standards of practice, code of ethics, and information on local care specialists by zip code. NAPGCM, 3275 W. Ina Road, Suite 130, Tucson, AZ 85741-2198, Phone 800-437-2423 or 301-948-3294 or go to www. caremanager.org. for information.

Note: Private franchises also offer families assistance in evaluating care needs and selecting care facilities. These for-profit enterprises may have contracts with specific care facilities, so choices may be confined to those facilities.

National Center for Assisted Living

"Assisted Living State Regulatory Review 2012." This publication documents twenty-one categories of information for each state, including pertinent regulations and programs pertaining to the care industry. Contact information is provided for state agencies that oversee assisted living activities. NCAL, 1201 L St. NW, Washington, DC 20005. Call 800-321-0342 or go to www.ahcancal.org.

NCAL also offers free consumer guides: Choosing an Assisting Living Residence, Moving into an Assisted Living Residence: Making a Successful Transition to Assisted Living, Caring for Someone with Alzheimer's, Having the Conversation About Long-Term Care, and Paying for Long-Term Care. Phone 800-628-8140 to order these publications.

Senior Companion Program

This program matches volunteers over age fifty-five with seniors who need help with finances, errands, or other activities that will help them remain independent in their own homes. Volunteers do not do personal care. For a list of local community organizations that offer this program, go to www.seniorcorps.gov and click on the "Senior Companions" box. Scroll down to lower-right state map titled "National Service in Your State" and click on name of state. Under "View your State" put in name of state. Click on "View Report," scroll down to Senior Corps and download "Senior Corps in (name of state).

Dancing with Rose

Author Lauren Kessler took an entry-level job at an Alzheimer's care facility to learn more about the devastating disease that claimed her mother. The story offers readers a dash of realism about life in a care facility from the viewpoint of both staff and residents. The story of life at the facility is interwoven with Kessler's journey of self-discovery about her relationship with her mother. For readers new to Alzheimer's and dementia, this readable book offers insights into personal relationships with dementia patients and care facilities. Lauren Kessler, *Dancing with Rose*, Viking, published by the Penguin Group, 375 Hudson Street, New York, NY 10014. Copyright © Lauren Kessler, 2007.

Chapter Three: Can We Afford a Care Facility?

Benefitscheckup.org

This is a free service of the National Council on Aging (NCOA). The Council's database identifies programs available for monetary assistance, including prescription medications, food, housing, transportation, in-home services, utilities, transportation, taxes, and health care. For information, contact NCOA, 1901 L Street, NW, Fourth Floor, Washington, DC 20036 or call 202-479-1200.

Metlife Mature Marketing Institute

"The 2012 MetLife Market Survey of Nursing Home, Assisted Living, Adult Day Services and Home Care Costs" analyzes statistics about populations in these facilities. Publication offers comparative information on nursing homes, assisted living, adult day care, and home care costs. MetLife Mature Marketing Institute, 57 Greens Farms Road, Westport, CT 06880. Phone 203-221-6580. To view the report online, go to www.metlife.com and type report title into search window.

National Association of Insurance Commission (NAIC) and the Center for Insurance and Policy Research

The NAIC has news releases and tips for consumers interested in purchasing long-term care insurance. Consumers can request a free publication titled *Shoppers Guide to Long-Term Care Insurance.* Contact NAIC customer service, phone 816-783-8300 or fax 816-460-7593. E-mail: prodserv@naic.org. Go to www.naic.org for further information.

Chapter Four: Care Facility Agreements

Genworth Financial, Inc.

The map on this website allows users to click on specific states and view median, annual long-term care costs for different types of care facilities. Type "maps-Genworth" in a Google search window or go to https://www.genworth.com/corporate/about-genworth/industry-expertise/state-maps.html. The "Genworth 2013 Cost of Care Survey" is also available on Genworth's website. The executive summary describes median monthly costs for all types of facilities, and discusses upward industry cost trends. Go to www.genworth.com and type the name of the report into the search window.

National Academy of Elderlaw Attorneys, Inc. (NAELA)

This website has contact information for state and local eldercare lawyers. Elder-law news, issues, library resources, brochures of specific elder-law topics and other information is available on the website. Call 703-942-5711 or go to www.naela.org/findlawyer.

National Adult Protective Services Association (NAPSA)

This website has contact information for state and local adult protective services offices. NAPSA offices provide education, services, and assistance to vulnerable adults who may be victims of abuse or neglect. NAPSA, 920 S. Spring Street, Springfield, IL 62704. Phone 217-523-4431 or e-mail info@napsa-now.org. Online, go to www.napsa-now.org and click on "help in your area, learn more" to pull up the interactive map. Click on a state for local contact information.

National Consumer Law Center (NCLC)

NCLC is a resource for locating low-income legal-services offices in states and local areas. See the Legal Services Corporation (LSC) directory, a nationwide directory of attorneys who assist low-income adults in civil (not criminal) matters. NCLC, 1001 Connecticut Avenue NW, Suite 510, Washington, DC 20036. Phone 202-452-6252 or visit www.nclc.org and click on tab "For Consumers, How to Get Legal Assistance" for a listing of services.

National Long-Term Care Ombudsman Resource Center

The resource center provides contact information for state, regional, and local ombudsman offices.

Ombudsman offices provide assistance with resolving complaints and problems consumers may have with care facilities. Go to www.ltcombudsman.org and click on "Locate an Ombudsman" on the map at the top right of web page. Write to: NORC, 1001 Connecticut Ave. NW, Suite 425, Washington, DC 20036. Phone 202-332-2275 or e-mail info@theconsumervoice.org.

National Senior Citizens Law Center

This nonprofit organization's principal mission is to protect the rights of low-income older adults. Its goal is to ensure the health and economic security of people through advocacy, litigation support, and education of local advocates. 1444 Eye Street NW, Suite 1100, Washington, DC 20005. Phone 202-289-6976 or visit www.nsclc.org.

Elder Care Locator

The eldercare locator is a public service of the US Administration on Aging. The eldercare locator website has fact sheets and brochures about issues faced by older adults and family caregivers. The website has links to other organizations and services. Eldercare Locator's goal is to help older adults and families identify trustworthy local support services and to offer information and resources that allow older adults to stay in their homes and communities as long as possible. Go to www.eldercare.gov or call 800-677-1116.

Chapter Five: Advocacy in Medical Care

Institute for Safe Medication Practices (ISMP)

ISMP has a wealth of information on care standards and industry issues about medication. A brochure titled

"America's Medicine Cabinet—Use Medications Safely," addresses the incorrect use of medications. Click on "Report Errors" tab and select "consumers/patients" to report medication errors. Institute for Safe Medication Practices, 200 Lakeside Drive, Suite 200, Horsham, PA 19044-2321. Call 215-947-7797 or go to www.ismp.org org.

Medline Plus

This National Institutes of Health website is a service of the National Library of Medicine. This website offers easy to understand consumer information about diseases, health, and wellness. Go to: www.nlm.nih.gov

The Alzheimer's Store

This online store offers books, training videos, and a full spectrum of care products for Alzheimer's and dementia patients. By mail: 425 Tribble Gap Road, Suite 209, Cumming, GA 3004. Phone 678-947-4001 or 800-752-3238. Fax 770-573-6808. Go to www.alzstore.com.

Chapter Six: Hospice and Palliative Care

Community Residential Care for the Frail Elderly: What Do We Know; What Should We Do?

The focus of this publication is on assisted living and adult family care. It talks about quality of life and affordability of residential care and discusses various models for service delivery. A literature review on related topics is available. This publication also covers topics such as privacy and nurse delegation. It makes future research recommendations. Although it is dated, it is an excellent preview of industry trends and findings relevant to the future wave of seniors who may have cognitive impairment. Larry Polivka

PhD, November 2006. Type the name of the study into a Google search window.

Hospice Patients Alliance

This organization offers a comprehensive list of topics about hospice, including how to choose a hospice program, standards of care, a description of the hospice team, financial resources available to pay for hospice, specific end-of-life care topics on pain control, and other useful subjects. Go to www.hospicepatients.org/maintopics.html.

Medicare and Hospice Benefits

Current information and publications on Medicare's hospice benefits are available by calling 800-633-4227. Go online to www.medicare.gov/publications for more information. Medicare lists two organizations that assist in locating state and local hospice organizations:

> National Hospice and Palliative Care Organization (NHPCO), 1731 King Street, Suite 100, Alexandria, VA 22314
> Phone 800-658-8898 or e-mail www.nhpco.org.

> Hospice Association of America, 228 Seventh Street SE, Washington, DC 20003
> Phone 202-546-4759 or e-mail: www.nahc.org

Chapter Seven: Advance Directives

Aging with Dignity

This organization offers information on the *Five Wishes®* living will. *Five Wishes®* offers a format for a living will with an array of personal choices about quality of life, emotional and spiritual matters, and end-of-life medical decisions not often included in traditional state living wills. It meets the legal requirements of forty-two states and the District of Columbia and is used in all fifty states. Aging with Dignity provides a link for consumers to order copies of the living will in English and other languages. Aging with Dignity, PO Box 1661, Tallahassee, FL 32302-1661. Call 888-594-7437 or go to www.fivewishes.org.

Caring Connections

This website of the National Hospice and Palliative Care Organization (NHPCO) allows users to download their state's advance directives. Note that forms can change or may be incorrect, and an in-state attorney should confirm that they meet all state current legal requirements at the time of signature. Online, go to www.caringinfo.org and click on "Download Your State's Specific Advance Directive." Call 800-658-8898 for NHPCO's help line.

Physician Orders for Life-Sustaining Treatment
Paradigm® (POLST)

The POLST website offers information about a comprehensive health-care form that allows seriously ill patients to document detailed information about their treatment wishes. Go to www.polst.org and click on "Find a Program in Your State." Go to "Resource Library" for examples of some state POLST forms and informational brochures, phone 503-494-3965 or write: National POLST Paradigm Task Force, Oregon Health & Science University, Center for Ethics in Health Care, 3181 SW Sam Jackson Park Road, Mail Code: UHN-86, Portland, Oregon 97239.

Health care and Elder Law Program Corporation (HELP)

This nonprofit organization provides information, education, and counseling on elder care, law, finances, and consumer protection. HELP offers private legal consultations (donation suggested), referrals, classes, and publications about current issues. Go to www.help4srs.com for specific information, or write to HELP, 1404 Cravens Avenue, Torrance, CA 90501. Phone 310-533-1996.

Chapter Eight: The Path Forward

The Eden Alternative

The Eden philosophy is based on a set of principles that guides facilities in changing ways they work with the elderly. Eden Alternative facilities demonstrate how patient-centered practices bring independence and dignity to residents. For more information about facilities that have adopted the Eden philosophy, write to the Eden Alternative, PO Box 18369, 1900 S. Clinton Avenue, Rochester, NY 14618. Phone 585-461-3951 or go to www.edenalt.org.

The Green House Project

The Green House philosophy has been adopted by a number of care facilities across the United States. The philosophy emphasizes homelike, resident-centered environments that support the dignity and privacy of Green House residents. Green House homes are built on a residential model, typically housing ten to twelve seniors, and they provide the full spectrum of skilled nursing care. The website discusses the philosophy and the goals of the Project and helps visitors locate Green House facilities.

The Green House Project, 2011 Crystal Dr., Arlington, VA 22202. Phone 703-647-2311 or e-mail greenhouse@ncb-capitalimpact.org. Go to http://thegreenhouseproject. org/about us and click on "Find a Home" for an interactive home locator map of the United States.

Elite Care

Elite Care—a resident-centered assisted living facility in Milwaukie, Oregon—offers seniors comfortable living suites in smaller buildings with central kitchens and living rooms. Elite Care provides on-site housing for some care staff, an unfamiliar twist in an industry with few incentive programs to combat employee turnover. The facility supplies 18 percent of its own food from onsite gardens and a chicken coop.

Elite Care's computer system monitors residents' private suites to detect changes in living patterns that might indicate medical problems. Residents and staff may wear clip-on badges to track locations as they move about the facility. The monitoring system uses infrared (IR) technology and radio frequency (RF) technology to identify locations. For information, contact Elite Care, 4444 SE Oatfield Hill Road, Milwaukie, OR 97267. Phone 503-742-4047 or go to www.elitecare.com.

The Pioneer Network

Founded in 1997 by a small group of long-term care professionals, the Pioneer Network's goal is to advocate for person-directed care and promote culture change in eldercare models. The website is a rich source of information about research, philosophy, and stories that explain the Pioneer Network's goals. The Pioneer Network is a not-for-profit organization. For information write: Pioneer Network, 35 East Wacker Drive, Suite

850, Chicago, IL 60601. Phone 312-224-2574 or go to www.pioneernetwork.net.

Technology information

Leading Age has a comprehensive report on the status and types of technologies available in today's market place to help seniors. Write: LeadingAge, 2519 Connecticut Avenue NW, Washington, DC 20008. Go to Google search window and type in "State of Technology in Aging Services Report," or go to www.leadingage.org/CAST.asp.

ENDNOTES

Introduction

1. National Institutes of Health estimates that 13.8 million people will have Alzheimer's disease or other dementias by the year 2050. The ranks of the very elderly—those eighty-five years and older and at the highest risk for Alzheimer's—are expected to triple by 2050. National Institutes of Health, Institute on Aging, "2011–2012 Alzheimer's Disease Progress Report."

Chapter One: Coming to Terms with Dementia

1. Alzheimer's Association. "What is Dementia?"
2. University of Western Sydney. "Dementia: Information for carers, friends, and families of people with severe and end-stage dementia."
3. ibid.
4. Encyclopedia of Mental Disorders, "Dementia: Causes."
5. Mark Kleinman, MD, interviewed by Brenda Niblock, Vancouver, WA, July 24, 2012.
6. Derick Scovel, PhD, Clinical Psychology, interviewed by Brenda Niblock, Vancouver, WA, August 1, 2012.

7. US Dept. of Health and Human Services. "Diagnosing Alzheimer's."
8. National Institutes of Health, Alzheimer Disease Education and Referral Center. "About Alzheimer's Disease: Diagnosis."
9. ibid.
10. Derick Scovel, op.cit.
11. Alzheimer's Association, "Types of Dementia."
12. This content was originally published by Caring.com: "Ten Types of Dementia That Aren't Alzheimer's and How They're Diagnosed." Excerpt reprinted here with permission.
13. Derick Scovel, op.cit.
14. ibid.
15. MedlinePlus, "Dementia."
16. Derick Scovel, op. cit.
17. HelpGuide.org. "Stages of Alzheimer's Disease." Used with permission from ©Helpguide.org. All rights reserved. Helpguide.org is an ad-free, non-profit resource for supporting better mental health and life-style choices for adults and children.
18. Ghent-Fuller, Jennifer. "Understanding the Dementia Experience," p. 24.
19. HelpGuide.org, op. cit.
20. ibid.
21. Derick Scovel, op. cit.
22. ibid.

Chapter Two: Care Facilities

1. National Center for Assisted Living (NCAL), "Assisted Living State Regulatory Review 2012." NCAL, 1201 L Street NW, Washington, DC 20005. www.nacal.org.

2. Facility and oversight monitoring varies from state to state. Each state is responsible for establishing its own licensing requirements. Agency for Healthcare Research and Quality (AHRQ), US Department of Health and Human Services, "Residential Care and Assisted Living."

3. Bessnette, David. "How to look up assisted living facility violations, citations and inspection reports," Enter the title in a Google search window to find the YouTube site.

4. The National Long-Term Care Ombudsman Resource Center is a portal to contact information to state and local long-term care ombudsman programs in all fifty states. See Information Resources at the end of this book for additional contact information. Go to www.ltcombudsman.org.

5. Goins, Toni, referral manager/marketing director, Liberty Country Place, interviewed by telephone by Pat Woodell, Centralia, WA, May 10, 2013.

6. Space requirements in adult family homes may vary from state to state.

7. There are two types of assistance: geriatric care specialists who work independently for the family and those (typically larger franchises) who have contracts with specific facilities. See the resource list at the end of the book for additional information.

8. The Resource section at the end of the book has several articles that address driving and dementia. They are intended to help families determine driving safety.

9. National Association of Area Agencies on Aging, 1730 Rhode Island Ave NW, Suite 1200, Washington, DC 20036. Phone 202-872-0888. State and local contact lists are available online at www.n4a.org. Find your local AAA or Title VI Native American aging program.

10. Visit the website of the National Association of Professional Geriatric Care Managers (NAPGCM) to view standards of practice, code of ethics, and local contact information. www.caremanager.org.
11. ibid.
12. Rendon, Jim. "Ten Things Assisted Living Homes Won't Tell You," Smart Money, p. 8.
13. National Center for Assisted Living, op. cit.
14. Teepa Snow is a dementia expert whose excellent videos provide living examples of the dementia viewpoint. http://www.YouTube.com/user/teepasnow. Also see Ghent-Fuller, "Understanding the Dementia Experience," September 27, 2003.

Chapter Three: The Advocate's Cash Planner

1. Rendon, Jim, "Ten Things Assisted Living Homes Won't Tell You," SmartMoney.
2. MetLife Mature Marketing Institute, "Market Survey of Long-Term Care Costs: The 2011 MetLife Market Survey of Nursing Home, Assisted Living, Adult Day Services, and Home Care Costs," October 2010. Statistics describe average monthly charges for different additional services like bathing ($307), dressing ($352), medication, toileting, eating and other expenses ($530), and medication management ($370). Statistics from other sources vary on percentages of people needing each service. People need the most help with medication, then bathing, followed by dressing, toileting, transferring, and eating.
3. See the Resource section at the end of the book for advisory literature from the National Association of

Insurance Commissioners and the NAIC Shoppers Guide to Long-Term Care Insurance.

4. The program is allowed in all fifty states as a result of the Deficit Reduction Act of 2005. See the US map at http://www.CompleteLongTermCare.com for links to information on state requirements for policies of participating insurance companies.

5. Administration on Aging, "What is Partnership Long-Term Care Insurance?"

6. National Council on Aging (NCOA). Go to www.ncoa.org and type "reverse mortgages" into the search window for a list of informative articles or write to NCOA Headquarters, 1901 L Street, NW, fourth floor, Washington, DC 20036. Phone 202-479-1200 or fax 202-479-0735.

7. Certner, David, legislative council and legislative policy director, government affairs in letter to Richard Cordray, Director, Bureau of Consumer Protection, "Request for Information Regarding Consumer Use of Reverse Mortgages," Docket No. CFPB-2012-0026.
AARP has expressed concerns about the need for full counseling before signing an agreement for a reverse mortgage. At the end of 2013, regulations changed amounts that can be borrowed.

8. Priority groups are based on income, length of military service, age, health, and other factors.

9. Available from http://www.seniorhomes.com/p/veterans-benefits/.

10. Contact the US Department of Veterans Affairs for information. www.va.gov/benefits/.

11. Contact www.seniorcare.com for an overview of the PACE program, a list of participating states, a list of services, and links to application information on the Medicare website.

12. US Department of the Treasury, Internal Revenue Service, Publication 502, Catalog No. 15002Q: "Medical and Dental Expenses."
13. See www.medicare.gov.
14. See Medicare booklet *Medicare and Home Health Care*, at http://www.medicare.gov/coverage/home-health-services.html.
15. Go to www.medicaid.gov.
16. Senior Assisted Housing Waiver: eligible residents of a state are offered choices of receiving care services at home or in a nursing facility. Each state has different allocations for room, board, and personal allowances.
17. Center for Medicare and Medicaid Services (CMS). "Medicaid Waivers." www.medicaid.gov/Medicaid-CHIP-Program-Information/By-Topics/waivers/waivers.HTML.
18. www.medicaid.gov/Medicaid-CHIP-Program-Information/By-State/By-State.html. Specific programs may include Community First Choice, State Balancing Incentive Program, and Money Follows the Person.
19. Genworth Financial, Inc., "Genworth 2013 Cost of Care Survey: Home Care Providers, Adult Day Health Care Facilities, Assisted Living Facilities and Nursing Homes, Tenth Edition."
    According to Genworth, there has been a 5.71 percent national increase in assisted living costs over the past five years.
20. Assisted Living Federation of America (ALFA), 1650 King Street, Suite 602, Alexandria, VA 22314. Phone 703-894-1805. More than half of assisted living facilities in the United States use a tiered-pricing model with bundled services.

21. Annual expenses are based on an estimated 4 percent increase in apartment rental and personal service costs.

22. MetLife Mature Marketing Institute, op. cit. This publication describes comparative cost information for in-home care and for living in various types of care facilities. Information varies by state.

23. ibid.

24. The American Elder Care Research Organization, PayingForSeniorCare.com. "Financial Assistance to Help Pay for or Reduce the Cost of Senior Living." Write to The American Elder Care Research Organization, 736 Cole Street, San Francisco, CA 94117. Phone 641-715-3900, ext. 60651 or go to www.payingforseniorcare.com.

25. See Family Caregiver Alliance, National Center on Care Giving at www.caregiver.org or contact Family Caregiver Alliance, 785 Market Street, Suite 750, San Francisco, CA 94103. Phone 415-434-3388 or 800-445-8106.

26. Family Caregiver Alliance, "Caregiving with Your Siblings." http://caregiver.org/caregiver/jsp/content_node.jsp?nodeid=2488 (accessed August 15, 2012).

27. Administration on Aging, Area Agencies on Aging.

Chapter Four: Care Facility Agreements

1. MetLife Mature Marketing Institute, op. cit. "Market Survey of Long-Term Care Costs—The 2010 MetLife Market Survey of Nursing Home, Assisted Living. Adult Day Care Services," October 2010.

2. Genworth Financial. op. cit. "Executive Summary—Genworth 2012 Cost of Care Survey Home Care Providers, Adult Day Health care Facilities, Assisted Living Facilities and Nursing Homes."

3. AssistedLivingFacilities.org. Accessed September 29, 2013. www.AssistedLivingFacilities.org/articles/assisted-living-costs.php.
4. An attorney-in-fact is a person who is named in a power of attorney (document) to act on the signer's behalf.
5. Checklists for skilled nursing facility care plans may differ.
6. Third party vendor is a contract term for a business or person who is mentioned in a contract but is not a party, or signer, to the contract.
7. Polzer, Karl, Senior Policy Director, "Assisted Living State Regulatory Review 2012," National Center for Assisted Living (NCAL), March 2012. This publication summarizes regulatory requirements. Contact regulatory oversight agencies listed in the report for the most current information.
8. National Long-Term Care Ombudsman Resource Center provides a portal to contact state, regional and local ombudsman offices. Go to www.ltcombudsman.org. Phone 800-677-1116.
9. National Adult Protective Services Association (NAPSA), links to state and regional Adult Protective Services offices. www.napsa-now.org or call 217-523-4431. E-mail info@napsa-now.org.
10. Polzer, op. cit. Identifies regulatory agencies responsible for overseeing assisted living facilities in each state.
11. Low-income facility residents can contact legal services center. Go to www.lsc.gov/find-legal-aid for information about local resources and income requirements to qualify for assistance. The National Senior Citizens Law Center (NSCLC) is a nonprofit organization whose principle mission is to protect rights of low-income older adults. www.nsclc.org. Private pay residents can

contact National Academy of Elder-Law Attorneys (NAELA) at www.naela.org/findlawyer.
12. Polzer, op. cit.

Chapter Five: Advocacy in Medical Care

1. Warning signs and cognitive tests for early dementia are described in Chapter One.
2. Institute for Safe Medication Practices (ISMP), "Ten Key Elements of Medication Delivery System." The institute offers information on a variety of issues related to standards in medical care. The publication can be used as a guideline to measure a facility's practices.
3. Grissinger, RPh, FASCP, "The Five Rights—A Destination Without a Map."
4. A proxy, or agent, is a person who acts on behalf of a patient in making medical decisions. This authority is granted in a document called a medical power of attorney, an advance care directive.
5. O'Conner, Anahad, "Four Drugs Cause Most Hospitalizations in Older Adults."
6. Washington Administrative Code 246-840-91-0979, "Delegation of Nursing Care Tasks in Community-Based and In-Home Care Settings."
7. US Department of Health and Human Services, Agency for Healthcare Research and Quality (AHRQ), "Residential Care and Assisted Living." Facility oversight and monitoring varies by state because each state is responsible for establishing its own licensing requirements.
8. There are seven major types of visual changes that may occur with cognitive decline, described in the following

reference: Bier, Deborah, PhD, "Improving Alzheimer's and Dementia Care: The Eyes Have it."

Chapter Six: Palliative Care

1. Reisberg, Barry, MD, New York University Medical Center's Aging and Dementia Research Center. Psychopharmacology Bulletin 1988:24:653-659. The FAST scale is designed to evaluate patients in more moderate to severe stages of dementia.
2. These programs have a variety of requirements that must be met to qualify for financial support. Information is available at Centers for Medicare & Medicaid Services (CMS), www.medicare.gov, CMS Publication No. 11361, July 11, 2011. For publications and information, phone 800-633-4227.
3. Local hospice organizations may also be found by contacting Hospice Association of America. Phone 202-546-4759 or go to www. nahc.org/haa, click on the "Consumers" tab, and go to Home Care and Hospice Locator. Enter the requested information and click "search," or click on a specific state on the map. Readers can also find hospice organizations by contacting Medicare. Not every hospice organization belongs to NAHC.
4. In 2010, 35 percent of hospice patients received services for seven days or less. NHPCO Facts and Figures-Hospice Care in America, 2011 Edition, P. 5. National Hospice and Palliative Care Organization, Alexandria, VA, www.nhpco.org. Phone 703-837-1500.
5. Facility residents are bathed on a set schedule. They don't receive daily baths.
6. " Alzheimer's Association, Greater Illinois Chapter. "Encouraging Comfort Care: A Guide for Families of

People with Dementia Living in Care Facilities 2010. Write to Greater Illinois Chapter, 8430 W. Bryn Mawr, Suite 800, Chicago, IL 60631. Phone 847-933-2413.

7. Karnes, Barbara, RN, *Gone From my Sight—The Dying Experience*, www.bkbooks.com.

8. Koepsell, Anne, MHQ, BSN, RN, Executive Director, Washington State Hospice and Palliative Care Organization, e-mail dated August 29, 2013.

9. Alzheimer's Association, Greater Illinois Chapter, op. cit., page 16.

Chapter Seven: Advance Care Planning

1. Medical Unit, ABC News. "Advance Care Planning: Take Charge of HOW You Die."

2. Alzheimer's Association, Greater Illinois Chapter, op. cit., page 11. Forcing intravenous (IV) fluids may lead to edema or swelling in the legs and difficulty breathing.

3. Examples of living wills are available for each state. Caring Connections, National Hospice and Palliative Care Organization (NHPCO), go to www.caringinfo. org.

4. Kutner, L., "Due Process of Euthanasia: The Living Will, a Proposal." *Indiana Law Journal* 44 (1969): 539.

5. NOLO Law for All, "Living Wills and Powers of Attorney for Health Care: An Overview," http://www.nolo.com/legal-encyclopedia/durable-power-of-attorney-health-finances-29579.html.

6. American Bar Association Commission on Law and Aging, "Default Surrogate Consent Statutes,2008." November 2009. www.americanbar.org. These statutes vary from state to state and are generally based on a federal, model surrogacy statute found in section 5 of the

Uniform Health-Care Decisions Act (UHDCA) (1993). The American Bar Association (ABA) review shows that forty-three states have enacted surrogacy statutes and seven states have not. The ABA listing shows the order of precedence for surrogates (spouse, children, etc.), standards for decision makers, if available, and other relevant information about each state's laws.

7. Caring Connections, National Hospice and Palliative Care Organization "Download Your State's Advance Directives," www.caringinfo.org. Phone 800-658-8898 or go to www.caringinfo@nhpco.org for more information.

8. National Academy of Elder Law Attorneys, Inc. Brochure: "Planning for Health Care Decision Making," copyright 2008. Contact www.NAELA.org or call 703-942-5711.

9. For information about *Five Wishes*, contact Aging with Dignity, PO Box 1661, Tallahassee, FL, 32302-1661. Phone 850-681-2010 or 888-594-7437 or e-mail fivewishes@agingwithdignity.org.

10. Silva, Mark, "Living Will With Heart Now Available," *Miami Herald*, July 24, 1997.

11. ibid.

12. Some states have different legal requirements for completing this form.

13. Ostrom, Carol M, "Bills Would Protect End-of-Life Decisions," *Seattle Times*, March 12, 2013. In some states, nuances of interpretation affect which medical personnel have legal backing to withhold or withdraw life-sustaining measures.

14. Although the US DOT has promulgated National EMS Education Standards (DOT HS 811 077A, January 2009), national guidelines for EMT training, specific

decisions about emergency procedures are often determined locally.

15. Cardiopulmonary resuscitation (CPR) is not advised for a person who has terminal dementia. If a person is frail, CPR can result in fractured ribs or other injuries. This may lead to other aggressive medical interventions, causing more pain and suffering for a person with advanced dementia.

16. Treatment measures included in out-of-hospital DNRs vary from state to state.

17. Zive, Dana M. and Schmidt, Terri A. "Pathways to POLST Registry Development: Lessons Learned," for National POLST Paradigm Task Force, The Retirement Research Foundation, Archstone Foundation, October 2012.

18. Federal law 42CFR489.102 requires care facilities and hospitals to have written policies and procedures about advance directives. Federal law also requires them to provide written information about advance directives for patients and their families (42 USC Section 1395 et seq.).

19. Terminal Patients' Right to Know End-of-Life Options Act. California Codes, health and safety code sections 442-442.7.

20. The Patient Self-Determination Act (PSDA) of 1990, 42 USC Section 1395 et seq.

21. "Consumer's Tool Kit for Health Care Advance Planning, Second Edition," American Bar Association (ABA) Commission on Law and Aging. Apps. americanbar.org/aging/publication.../consumer_tool_kit_bk.p.

22. Dunn, Hank, "Hard Choices for Loving People—CPR, Artificial Feeding, Comfort Care & the Patient with

a Life-Threatening Illness," Accessed Sept. 26, 2012. www.hankdunn.com. Used with permission of author.
23. ibid. p. 52.

Chapter Eight: The Path Forward

1. See the resources section for more information about the Pioneer movement.
2. Transitional-care patients are skilled nursing patients who are living in a care facility until they recover from surgery, broken bones, or other short-term medical conditions.
3. For more information about the *Eden Alternative*, visit www.edenalt.org or write PO Box 18369, 1900 S. Clinton Avenue, Rochester, NY 14618. Phone 585-461-3951 or fax 585-244-9114.
4. Dorothy Boyd, RN, ADNS, assistant director of nursing, interviewed by Pat Woodell at Liberty Country Place, Centralia, WA, March 16, 2012.
5. For a list of available Green House homes in each state, go to www.thegreenhouseproject.org. Click on "Find a Home" tab to bring up a map of the United States.
6. Fenswick, Carla and Gilmer, Lillian. "Examining the Green House Project Senior Living Concept," *Nashville Business Journal* (March 5, 2006).
7. Elite Care: see the Resources section for a detailed description of the facility.
8. Neergaard, Lauran, The Associated Press, "One in Seven Patients with Alzheimer's Lives Alone," *Tacoma News Tribune* (May 14, 2012).
9. A variety of informative safety tips and tools are available for those living at home or in assisted living apartments. www.thiscaringhome.com.

10. Seattle, WA, "Aging Your Way" sponsored a series of neighborhood meetings in 2011. These meetings discussed ideas for integrating communities and increasing services to those in need. www.seniorservices.org/agingyourway/Home.aspx.
11. Beacon Hill Village, located in Boston, MA, started with 450 members in 2001. www.beaconhillvillage.org.
12. An organization called North East Seattle Together (NEST) opened its doors on May 1, 2012. Its goal is to help seniors remain in their homes longer by providing local community support. A membership fee is required. www.nestseattle.org.
13. Snyder, Arnie, "The Village Movement and the 2010 National Village Gathering."
14. "Quick Facts about Programs of All-Inclusive Care for the Elderly (PACE)." Http://www.medicare.gov/Pubs/pdf/11341.pdf. See chapter 3 for additional information.
15. Fernandes, Edna, "Dementiaville: How an experimental new town is taking the elderly back to their happier and healthier pasts with astonishing results."
16. Aldersgate—A United Methodist Retirement Community, Cuthbertson Village at Aldersgate, Charlotte, NC.
17. See Appendix 3, Technologies—Now and the Future, for a brief description of these technologies.
18. The ORCATECH Living Lab is a community-based group of volunteer seniors who have agreed to participate in testing emerging technologies in their homes. For more information, go to www.orcatech.org.

Appendix 1: Cognitive Testing

1. Reproduced by special permission of the publisher, Psychological Assessment Resources, Inc., 16204 North Florida Avenue, Lutz, Florida 33549, from the Mini-Mental State Examination, by Marshal F. Folstein, MD and Susan E. Folstein, MD. Copyright 1975, 1998, 2001 by Mini-Mental LLC, Inc.
2. UK Alzheimer's Society. "The Mini-Mental State Examination (MMSE)."
3. Tariq, S. H., Tumosa, N., Chibnall, J. T., et al, "Comparison of the Saint Louis University Mental Status Examination and the Mini-Mental State Examination for detecting dementia and mild neurocognitive disorder: a pilot study."
4. O'Bryant, Sid E., Humphreys, Joy D., et al. "Detecting Dementia with the Mini-Mental State Examination (MMSE) in Highly Educated Individuals."
5. Tariq S. H., et al., op. cit.

Appendix 2: Care-Plan Costs: The Point System in Assisted Living and Memory Care Facilities

1. Two facilities told us the unit of time for a point is based on six minutes. Most articles on the subject discuss points in terms of overall cost for each type of service (for example, medication at $180/month) rather than units of time.
2. The term "full care" is generally understood to mean that the person cannot perform the activities of daily

living (ADLs) without assistance. The ADLs include: walking, toileting, dressing, eating, and transferring. Full-care patients may need additional services such as grooming, dental hygiene, and so forth.

BIBLIOGRAPHY

ABC News Medical Unit. "Advance Care Planning: Take Charge of HOW You Die." *ABC News.* http://abcnews. go.com/blogs/health/2012/08/22/advance-care-planning-take-charge-of-how-you-die (accessed August 22, 2012).

Administration on Aging. "Eldercare Locator." *Eldercare. gov.* http://www.eldercare.gov/Eldercare.NET/Public/Index.aspx (accessed September 21, 2013).

—. "What is Partnership Long-Term Care Insurance." *Longtermcare.gov.* http://longtermcare.gov/medicare-medicaid-more/state-based-programs (accessed Aug-ust 15, 2012).

Aging Home Health Care, "Early Treatment Dementia Test: St. Louis Mental Status Exam." http://www. aginghomehealthcare.com/treatment-dementia-2.ht (accessed August 31, 2012).

Aging with Dignity. "Five Wishes." *Aging with Dignity.* http://www.agingwithdignity.org (accessed September 22, 2012).

Agingcare.com. "Veteran Assistance for Alzheimer's and Dementia Care." *AgingCare.* www.agingcare.com/articles/vet-assistance-for-Alzheimer-s-and-Dementia-Care-136878.htm (accessed July 24, 2012).

Aldersgate—A United Methodist Retirement Community. "Cuthbertson Village at Aldersgate." *Aldersgate CCRC.* www.aldersgateccrc.com/health-care-options/memory-care (accessed August 28, 2013).

Alzheimer's Association. 2012 Alzheimer's Disease Facts and Figures, Alzheimer's & Dementia, Volume 8, Issue 2. Alzheimer's Association, 2012.

—. "Types of Dementia." *alz.org.* http://www.alz.org/dementia/types-of-dementia.asp (accessed September 9, 2013).

—. "What is Dementia?" *alz.org.* http:// www.alz.org/what-is-dementia.asp (accessed September 4, 2012).

Alzheimer's Association, Greater Illinois Chapter. "Encouraging Comfort Care: A Guide for Families of People with Dementia Living in Care Facilities 2010." http://www.ccal.org/eldercare-and-disability/alzheimers-dementia (accessed September 26, 2012).

American Bar Association Commission on Law and Aging. "Consumer's Tool Kit for Health Care Advance Planning, Second Edition." *American Bar Association.* http://www.americanbar.org/groups/law_aging/resources/consumer_s_toolkit_for_health_care_advance_planning.html (accessed April 21, 2013).

—. "Default Surrogate Consent Statutes." *American Bar Association.* November 2009. http://www.americanbar.org/content/dam/aba/migrated/aging/PublicDocuments/famcon_2009.authcheckdam.pdf (accessed April 21, 2013).

American Elder Care Research Organization. "Financial Assistance to Help Pay for or Reduce the Cost of Senior Living." *Paying for Senior Care.* www.payingforseniorcare.com/longtermcare/paying-for-assisted-living.html#D6 (accessed July 24, 2012).

AssistedLivingFacilities.org. *AssistedLivingFacilities.org.* www.AssistedLivingFacilities.org/articles/assisted-living-costs.php (accessed September 29, 2013).

Australian Government, Department of Health and Ageing. "Supporting Australians to Live Well at the End of Life—National Palliative Care Strategy 2010." *Australian Government, Department of Health.* 2010. http://www.health.gov.au/internet/main/publishing.nsf/Content/palliativecare-strategy.htm (accessed November 1, 2012).

Bessnette, David. "How to look up assisted living facility violations, citations, and inspection reports." *YouTube.* http://www.youtube.com/watch?v=SxuxvCWc4-k (accessed May 26, 2011).

Bier, Deborah, PhD. "Improving Alzheimer's and Dementia Care: The Eyes Have it." *Psych Central.* http://www.psychcentral.com/lib/improving-alzheimers-and-dementia-care-the-eyes-have-it/00013200 (accessed January 12, 2013).

Boyd, Dorothy, RN, ADNS, Assistant Director of Nursing, interview by Pat Woodell. Centralia, WA (March 16, 2012).

California State Legislature. "Right to Know End-of-Life Options Act." *California Codes, health and safety code sections 442-442.7.*

Caring Connections. "Download Your State's Advance Directives." *Caring Connections.* http://www.caringinfo.org/i4a/pages/index.cfm?pageid=3289 (accessed April 21, 2013).

Caring.com. "Ten Types of Dementia That Aren't Alzheimer's and How They're Diagnosed." *Caring.com.* http://www.caring.com/articles/dementia-diagnosing-tests (accessed September 9, 2013). This excerpt is reprinted here with permission.

Centers for Medicare and Medicaid Services (CMS). *Medicare and Home Health Care.* July 11, 2011.

—. *Waivers, CMS Publication No. 11361.* July 11, 2011. http://www.medicaid.gov. For publications and information, call 1-800-633-4227.

—. Medicare and Hospice Benefits, CMS Publication No. 11361. July 11, 2011.

Certner, David, Legislative Counsel and Legislative Policy Director, Government Affairs, on behalf of AARP. "Request for Information Regarding Consumer Use of Reverse Mortgages, Docket No. CFPB-2012-0026, letter to Bureau of Consumer Financial Protection." *AARP.* http://www.aarp.org/content/dam/aarp/politics/advocacy/2012-09/reverse-mortgage-request-for-info-cfpb2012-rev0827.pdf (accessed August 31, 2012).

Colorado Bar Association. "The Patient Self-Determination Act (PSDA) of 1990. 42 USC Section 1395 et seq." *Colorado Bar Association.* http://www.cobar.org/index.cfm/ID/1816/subID/6626/CLPE/Summary-of-the-Patient-Self-Determination-Act-from-the-Commission-on-Law-and-Aging-at-the-ABA (accessed September 21, 2013).

Dunn, Hank. *Hard Choices for Loving People: CPR, Artificial Feeding, Comfort Care and the Patient with a Life-Threatening Illness.* Herndon, VA: A & A Publishers, Inc., 2004. Copies can be ordered online at http://www.hank-dunn.com. Used with permission of author.

Encyclopedia of Mental Disorders. "Dementia: Causes." *Encyclopedia of Mental Disorders.* http://www.minddisorders.com/Del-Fi/Dementia.html (accessed August 12, 2013).

Family Caregiver Alliance. "Other Web Resources." *Family Caregiver Alliance.* http://www.caregiver.org/caregiver/

jsp/content_node.jsp?nodeid=354 (accessed January 19, 2013).

Fenswick, Carla, and Lillian Gilmer. "Examining the Green House Project Senior Living Concept." *Nashville Business Journal* (March 5, 2006).

Fernandes, Edna. "Dementiaville: How an experimental new town is taking the elderly back to their happier and healthier pasts with astonishing results." *MailOnline* (March 4, 2012).

Folstein, MD, Marshal F., and Susan E. Folstein, MD. "The Mini-Mental State Examination." Lutz, FL: Psychological Assessment Resources, 2001. Further reproduction is prohibited without permission of PAR, Inc. The MMSE can be purchased from PAR, Inc. by calling 813-968-3003.

Ghent-Fuller, Jennifer. "Understanding the Dementia Experience." Cambridge, Ont.: Alzheimer's Society Cambridge, 2003.

Goins, Toni, referral manager/marketing director, interview by Pat Woodell. Centralia, WA, (March 16, 2012).

Grissinger, RPh, FASCP. "The Five Rights—A Destination Without a Map." *Pharmacy and Therapeutics (P&T)* 35 (2010): 542. http://www.ncbi.nlm.nih.gov/pmc/articles/ PMC2957754/#__ffn_sectitle (accessed September 21, 2013).

HelpGuide.org. "Stages of Alzheimer's Disease." *Helpguide. org.* http://www.helpguide.org/elder/alzheimers_disease_symptoms_stages.htm. Used with permission from ©Helpguide.org. (accessed September 25, 2012).

Institute for Safe Medication Practices (ISMP). "Ten Key Elements of a Medication Delivery System." *Institute for Safe Medication Practices (ISMP).* http://www.ismp.org/ faq (accessed September 21, 2013).

Karnes, Barbara, RN. *Gone From My Sight: The Dying Experience.* Vancouver, WA: Barbara Karnes Books, Inc., 2008. This booklet can be ordered online at http://www.bkbooks.com.

Kleinman, Mark, MD. interview by Brenda Niblock. Vancouver, WA, (July 24, 2012).

Koepsell, Anne, MHQ, BSN, RN, Executive Director, Washington State Hospice and Palliative Care Organization, e-mail message to Pat Woodell. (August 29, 2013).

Kulick, Daniel Lee, MD, FACC, FSCAI. "Congestive Heart Failure." *On Health.* http://www.onhealth.com/congestive_heart_failure/article.htm (accessed September 21, 2013).

Kutner, Luis. "Due Process of Euthanasia: The Living Will: A Proposal." *Indiana Law Journal* 44, no. 4 (1969). http://www.repository.law.indiana.edu/ilj/vol44/iss4/2 (accessed September 21, 2013).

Library of Congress. "The Patient Self-Determination Act (PSDA) of 1990," 42 USC Section 1395 et seq." http://thomas.loc.gov/cgi-bin/query/z?c101:H.R.4449.IH: (accessed September 21, 2013).

MedLine Plus. "Dementia." *MedLine Plus.* MD: National Library of Medicine (US) Bethesda. September 26, 2011. http://www.nlm.nih.gov/medlineplus/ency/article/000739.htm (accessed April 24, 2013).

MetLife Mature Marketing Institute. "Market Survey of Long-Term Care Costs, The 2010 MetLife Market Survey of Nursing Home, Assisted Living, Adult Day Services and Home Care Costs." October 2010. https://www.metlife.com/assets/cao/mmi/publications/studies/2011/mmi-market-survey-nursing-home-assisted-living-adult-day-services-costs.pdf (accessed September 21, 2013).

National Academy of Elder-Law Attorneys, Inc. (NAELA). "Planning for Health Care Decision Making." *National Academy of Elder-Law Attorneys, Inc. (NAELA).* http:// naela.epmonline.com/images/1/25-75315900/ HCDM.pdf (accessed April 21, 2013).

—. "Provisions for Long-Term Care at Home." *National Academy of Elder-Law Attorneys, Inc. (NAELA).* http:// www.naela.epmonline.com/images/1/25-75315900/ PLTC.pdf (accessed September 21, 2013).

National Association of Professional Geriatric Care Managers, NAPGCM, 3275 W. Ina Road, Suite 130, Tucson, AZ 85741-2198, Phone 800-437-2423 or 301-948-3294 or go to www.caremanager.org. (accessed April 25, 2013).

National Center for Assisted Living (NCAL). "Assisted Living State Regulatory Review 2012." *National Center for Assisted Living (NCAL).* 2012. http://www.ahcancal. org/ncal/resources/Pages/AssistedLivingStudies.aspx (accessed March 15, 2013).

National Council on Aging. "Reverse Mortgages." *National Council on Aging.* http://www.ncoa.org/about-ncoa/ locations.html#sthash.XM1zyUeW.dpuf (accessed August 15, 2013).

National Hospice & Palliative Care Organization. "Caring for Persons with Alzheimer's and Other Dementias— Guidelines for Hospice Providers." *National Hospice & Palliative Care Organization.* May 2008. http://www. nhpco.org/resources-access-outreach/dementia-resources (accessed September 21, 2013).

—. "NHPCO Facts & Figures—Hospice Care in America, 2011 Edition." *National Hospice & Palliative Care Organization.* http://www.nhpco.org/resources-access-outreach/ dementia-resources (accessed September 21, 2013).

National Institutes of Health, Alzheimer Disease Education and Referral Center. "About Alzheimer's Disease: Diagnosis." *National Institute on Aging*. http://www.nia.nih.gov/alzheimers/topics/diagnosis (accessed August 31, 2012).

National Institutes of Health, Institute on Aging. "2011–2012 Alzheimer's Disease Progress Report." *National Institute on Aging*. http://www.nia.nih.gov/alzheimers/publication/2011-2012-alzheimers-disease-progress-report/introduction#looming (accessed September 21, 2013).

National Long-Term Care Ombudsman Resource Center. "Locate an Ombudsman, State Agencies and Citizen Advocacy Groups." *The National Long-Term Care Ombudsman Resource Center*. http://www.ltcombudsman.org/ombudsman (accessed September 21, 2013).

Neergaard, Lauran. "One in Seven Patients with Alzhimer's Lives Alone." *Tacoma News Tribune*, May 14, 2012.

NOLO Law for All. "Living Wills and Powers of Attorney for Health Care: An Overview." *NOLO*. http://www.nolo.com/legal-encyclopedia/living-will-power-of-attorney-29595.html (accessed September 21, 2013).

O'Bryant, Sid E., Joy D. Humphreys, et al. "Detecting Dementia with the Mini-Mental State Examination (MMSE) in Highly Educated Individuals." 2008. doi:10.1001/archneur.65.7.963 (accessed August 6, 2013).

O'Conner, Anahad. "Four Drugs Cause Most Hospitalizations in Older Adults." *New York Times*. November 23, 2011. http://well.blogs.nytimes.com/2011/11/23/four-drugs-cause-most-hospitalizations-in-older-adults/?_r=0 (accessed September 21, 2013).

ORCATECH Living Lab. "LeadingAge, Center for Aging Services Technologies (CAST)." *ORCA Tech*. www.orcatech.org (accessed August 18, 2013).

Ostrom, Carol M. "Bills Would Protect End-of-Life Decisions." *Seattle Times.* March 12, 2013. http://seattletimes.com/html/localnews/2020537263_cprnocprxml.html.

Otto, Allyson, and Garon Primmer, interview by Pat Woodell, Brenda Niblock and Jeri Warner. Milwaukie, OR (September 6, 2013).

Program of All-Inclusive Care for the Elderly (PACE). "Quick Facts about Programs of All-Inclusive Care for the Elderly (PACE)." *Medicare.* http://www.medicare.gov/Pubs/pdf/11341.pdf (accessed August 28, 2013).

Reisberg, Barry, MD. "Functional Assessment Staging (FAST)." *Psychopharmacology Bulletin* 24 (1988): 653-659 http://www.everydayhealth.com/alzheimers (accessed September 21, 2013).

Rendon, Jim. *Ten things assisted-living homes won't tell you.* March 4, 2013. http://marketwatch.com.

Scovel, Derick, PhD, interview by Brenda Niblock. Vancouver, WA, (August 1, 2012).

Senior Services. "Aging Your Way." *Senior Services.* www.seniorservices.org/agingyourway/Home.aspx (accessed August 18, 2013).

Silva, Mark. "Living Will with Heart Now Available." *Miami Herald,* July 24, 1997.

Snyder, Arnie. "The Village Movement and the 2010 National Village Gathering." *Senior Resource Guide.* http://www.seniorsresourceguide.com/articles/art01003.html (accessed March 15, 2012).

Social Security Administration, Center for Medicare and Medicaid Services (CMS). "Medicaid Waivers." *Medicaid.* www.medicaid.gov/Medicaid-CHIP-Program-Information/By-Topics/Waivers/WaiversHTML (accessed September 29, 2013).

Tariq, S. H., N. Tumosa, J. T. Chibnall, et al. "Comparison of the Saint Louis University Mental Status Examination and the Mini-Mental State Examination for detecting dementia and mild neurocognitive disorder: a pilot study." *American Journal of Psychiatry* 14 (2006): 900–910 (accessed Sept. 4, 2012. http://www.ncbi.nlm.nih.gov/pubmed/17068312).

UK Alzheimer's Society. "The Mini-Mental State Examination (MMSE)." *UK Alzheimer's Society.* http://www.alzheimers.org.uk/site/scripts/documents_info.php?documentID=121 (accessed September 4, 2012).

University of Western Sydney. "Dementia: Information for carers, friends, and families of people with severe and end-stage dementia." *University of Western Sydney.* Palliative Care Dementia Interface: Enhancing Community Capacity Project. 2011. http://www.uws.edu.au/__data/assets/pdf_file/0008/7100/Dementia_Booklet_Final2011_PDFfor_web.pdf (accessed September 4, 2012).

US Department of Health and Human Services. "Diagnosing Alzheimer's." *Alzheimers.gov.* http://www.alzheimers.gov/diagnosing.html (accessed September 4, 2012).

US Department of Health and Human Services, Agency for Healthcare Research & Quality (AHRQ). "Residential Care and Assisted Living." *Agency for Healthcare Research and Quality.* http://www.ahrq.gov/research/findings/final-reports/residentcare/index.html (accessed September 21, 2013).

Washington State Legislature. "Delegation of Nursing Care Tasks in Community-Based and In-Home Care Settings, Washington Administrative Code 246-840-91-0970." *Washington State Legislature.* http://apps.leg.wa.gov/

rcw/default.aspx?cite=18.79.260 (accessed August 15, 2013).

Zive, Dana M., and Terri A. Schmidt. "Pathways to POLST Registry Development: Lessons Learned." *POLST.* Archstone Foundation, the Retirement Research Foundation. October 2012. http://www.polst.org/wp-content/uploads/2012/12/POLST-Registry.pdf (accessed September 21, 2013).